Persecution of the Church

Don McAlvany

Persecution of the Church
Copyright © 1993 by Don McAlvany

This material is for the glory of Jesus Christ.
We encourage its distribution.

Published by:
Southwest Radio Church
P.O. Box 1144
Oklahoma City, OK 73101
(405) 235-5396
1-800-652-1144 ● FAX (405) 236-4634

ISBN 1-879366-36-3

Table of Contents

Introduction

"The strength or weakness of a society depends more on the level of its spiritual life than on its level of industrialization. Neither a market economy nor even general abundance constitutes the crowning achievement of human life. If a nation's spiritual energies have been exhausted, it will not be saved from collapse by the most perfect government structure or by any industrial development. A tree with a rotten core cannot stand" (Alexander Solzhenitsyn).

"When the righteous are in authority, the people rejoice: but when the wicked beareth rule, the people mourn" (Prov. 29:2).

There is a black cloud rolling across America. The great majority of Americans cannot even see it as they live on in a contented, complacent comfort zone that sees no evil, hears no evil, and feels no evil. There are powerful forces at work in America today which have a well-strategized design to move America into a socialist police state and the New World Order.

These forces have been accelerating tremendously over the past five years and especially over the past six months. They believe that there is virtually no resistance to their plan to subjugate the American people into their globalist vision of *"a world that will be as one," by the year 2000.*

Certainly there is *no resistance* from a Congress or judiciary which goes along with 98 percent of the agenda the Establishment has for America. There is *no resistance* from the media, which is a not-so-silent partner to the Establishment in keeping the American people asleep, and psychologically preparing them for Global 2000 and the dawning of the Age of Aquarius.

There is *no resistance* from the churches of America which are also in a very complacent comfort zone. *It is as if a spirit of blindness or delusion has settled over Americans in general and the Christian Church in particular,* and as the affronts, insults, and attacks against our traditional, Constitutional, and biblical values grow every day, almost geometrically, the average Christian in America goes even more deeply to sleep.

And there is *no resistance* from the American population which continues in its comfort zone of affluence as the government and media hypnotize, mesmerize, and pacify them, even as America descends into an economic, social, political, moral, and spiritual free fall. *America is much like Nazi Germany in the late 1920s and early '30s--in moral, spiritual, and political decline, and psychologically ripe to accept the New World Order.*

But there is some resistance from a small handful of Americans (probably no more than two million) who *do* see the moral, spiritual, social, free fall which America is in today, who *do* recognize the evil emanating from Washington, our courts, our media, and our educational system. This remnant of Americans is waking up to (or is fully aware of) the danger America and our entire way of life faces over the next three to seven years.

Some of this remnant are conservatives, some are Christians, a few are Jewish, a few liberal, some are home schoolers, many are gun owners. Whatever the religious or political persuasion of this remnant, *they have* discernment about the dangers America faces, *they have* a love for our traditional way of life, and *they have* a loathing (or hatred) for evil.

It is this remnant, this potential resistance to the socialization and globalization of America, which the Establishment most fears and hates at this point. If this remnant were to suddenly grow from a few million to 25 to 50 to 75 to 100 million Americans, the Establishment's New World Order/ New Age blueprint for America would go up in smoke--and the Establishment knows it. *This remnant, and the intervening hand of God, are the only things which can reverse America's present free fall and plunge into slavery.* So, they must move to stamp out the remnant, the dissidents, the potential resistance--as swiftly, totally, and ruthlessly as Lenin, Stalin, Hitler, and Mao did as they were rising to power in the '20s, '30s, '40s, and '50s.

This book is about the coming persecution of the remnant. It has begun. The siege at Ruby Creek against the Weaver family and Operation Waco will be seen in retrospect as watershed events in the government's escalating attacks against the remnant. The Waco massacre and America's accelerating plunge toward a police state and the New World Order will be analyzed in detail.

Chapter One

Tracking Americans:
The Growing Elimination of Privacy

Just as in George Orwell's *1984*, "Big Brother's" machinery for tracking and monitoring every American citizen continues to grow. The FDIC is about to implement a system for tracking the deposits of *all* Americans in *all* financial institutions. Once installed, a major part of your financial privacy will be almost totally eliminated.

One of the most dangerous aspects of the Clinton Administration is its hatred of privacy. Under the pretense of national health care reform, the Clinton's are moving to implement what Clinton and Gore talked about in their campaign book *Putting People First*: "*smart cards for everyone coded with personal medical information.*"

The National Identification Card

The new card will be the size of a credit card; it will be issued at birth; it will have embedded in it a computer with a memory chip and microprocessor with up to 1,600 pages of personal information on its owner, which will be sufficient for a complete dossier on the entire lives of most American citizens. No one will get "official" medical care unless he presents the card.

Martin Anderson, a former official with the Reagan White House wrote on April 4, 1993 in the *Washington Times*:

"*Brushing aside any concerns about personal privacy, a powerful array of government agencies (i.e., the Immigration and Naturalization Service, the State Department, the FBI, the IRS, the CIA, etc.), each with its own special reasons, lusted after a law to force every American to carry a national identity card. Such a law was within a whisker of being endorsed by Mr.*

Reagan's Cabinet in 1981, and was stopped only when the President personally vetoed the idea on the grounds that it was a massive invasion of privacy."

Today, twelve years later, there is virtually no resistance to the card. Ira Magaziner, Hillary's socialized medicine czar (a socialist who wrote a book on the glories of socialism called *Minding America's Business*) is spearheading the drive for a national computerized ID card. It will eventually include your tax history; how many cars you own; the number and kind of guns you own; data on your children; your history of addresses and phone numbers; any dealings with any federal agency; your electronic photo; your fingerprints; and, of course, your medical history and much more. The FBI has already signed a contract with Harris Corporation of Melbourne, Florida to give the government the electronic fingerprint capacity.

As Martin Anderson recently wrote:

"Unless this national ID card is stopped quickly, we may live to see the end of privacy in the U.S., all of us tagged like so many fish. Of course, the argument goes, 'if you have nothing to hide, you should not be concerned.' And, hey, you don't have anything to hide, do you?"

Part of the Clintonista push for the ID card will also be, "Don't you want better health care at a lower cost? Then you have to have computerized medical records."

Toward a Cashless Society

The government is proceeding quickly to move us toward a cashless computerized society. It has now proposed a $1 coin to replace the $1 bill. (Through a series of accounting tricks, the government claims that the cost savings would be $395 million per year. But they have manufactured these numbers just as they have the unemployment, GDP, and inflation numbers.)

The proposal by the General Accounting Office also suggests that *"the coin's size should be determined considering the future possibility of higher denomination coins, such as $2 and $5 coins."* This GAO recommendation should be considered in the context of other government recommendations to eliminate $50 and $100 bills.

The ultimate government goal is the abolition of all cash and the luring of Americans into the computerized banking, credit card, or "smart card" system. The incredible inconvenience of carrying around $20, or $50, or $100, or $200 in heavy coins is deemed by our government planners to be enough cause to turn most people to plastic credit or "smart" cards. Most people will use the bank debit card for purchases, and the poor will use their government-issued credit cards as they are already doing in some states.

The Day of the "Smart Card"

A major push is about to be launched by the Establishment to persuade the American public to forego their cash and begin using the so-called "smart card." Typical of the sales pitch is an article in the *Wall Street Journal* (May 10, 1993) entitled "Someday, Cards May Make Coins Obsolete." Arguments are presented such as:

1. "You never have enough coins when you need them to buy newspapers from vending machines."
2. "When you make small purchases, change always comes in pennies, and they rattle in your pocket."
3. "It is hard to fish out change on a toll road, but, with the 'smart card' you'll never be caught short of change."
4. "'Smart cards' eliminate vandalism and theft at vending machines."
5. "Convenience stores open at night can reduce the threat of robbery by using and accepting 'smart cards' only after dark, instead of cash."

The *Wall Street Journal* article discusses college students who are using college-issued "electronic purses" (i.e., simple "smart cards") in soda machines, library copiers, dormitory laundries, and even cafeterias, citing the "greater convenience." The use of "smart cards" for parking meters and bus fares is being highly touted in the article; and the use of "smart cards" by the Marine trainees at the Parris Island boot camp in South Carolina for all cash transactions is discussed.

The "smart card" is a vital part of moving Americans toward a cashless society, which is a major element of the coming New World Order. Readers should avoid the use of "smart cards" unless privacy and government control of your life is of no concern to you. As Nancy Reagan used to say: *"Just say no!"*

Chapter Two

Plunging Toward an American Police State

Government Seizures and Forfeitures Continue to Accelerate

The January '93 issue of *McAlvany Intelligence Advisor* discussed the government's draconian (and unconstitutional) seizure/forfeiture laws, and how local, state, and federal government agencies are seizing the assets of innocent law-abiding Americans at a rate of about 1,000 seizures per week (totalling over $800 million in 1992) for alleged violations of cash reporting, environmental, medical, child abuse, safety, tax, and other regulations. *Although these seizures are receiving growing publicity, the number of seizures and amounts of assets being seized is continuing to grow and there is no evidence of a cessation of the trend. In fact, all over the country, law enforcement officials are being trained in how to make more efficient, more effective, and more profitable seizures.* Several recent government attacks on citizens are illustrative:

Paul and Rosie Berger, Sand Springs, Montana

At 6:00 a.m., Wednesday, March 25, 1993, more than 20 federal law enforcement agents of the U.S. Fish and Wildlife Service and the Bureau of Land Management (armed and wearing bulletproof vests) invaded the ranch of Paul and Rosie Berger (aged 84 and 91) near Sand Springs, Montana. The agents, armed with a search warrant and seizure authority signed by the U.S. magistrate in Great Falls, descended on the Berger sheep and cattle ranch to look for evidence of eagle poisoning. A disgruntled ex-employee had accused the Bergers of poisoning eagles.

The agents seized two Chevrolet pickup trucks belonging to the Bergers, as well as farm chemicals and other equipment. *While Berger and his wife were being questioned for over six hours and their property searched by the federal agents, the Bergers were not advised of their rights and were not allowed to call an attorney.* For almost six hours, the Feds would not allow any lawyers, neighbors, or local reporters onto the property. There are several interesting aspects to the unconstitutional government seizure:

1. The federal agents took a CNN television crew in with them on the raid--obviously desiring national television coverage if anything juicy was uncovered (just as they did in the initial BATF attack against the Branch Davidian compound in Waco. The public relations coordinator for CNN later issued a statement adamantly denying that their raid was staged for CNN's cameras).

2. The Feds completely circumvented the local sheriff's department before and during the raid, totally blowing off any local or county jurisdiction in the so-called "investigation."

3. *Poisoning eagles is now a federal crime--punishable by jail, fines, and/or confiscation of property, whether or not the poisoning is accidental or intentional.* [**Note:** Many western ranchers are plagued by coyotes, wolves, and other predators who prey upon their herds and their livelihood. For almost 150 years it has been traditional throughout the west that ranchers can protect their herds from wild animals. Hence, they hunt, trap, and poison such predators. *But now, if they accidentally poison an eagle they can lose their property and go to jail-- another byproduct of our present environmental insanity.*]

4. The informant (a disgruntled ex-employee) will receive a 10 to 25 percent finder's fee on any assets confiscated and ultimately sold at a government forfeiture auction (which for disgruntled ex-employees may be ultimately much more profitable than working for a living).

Ed Jacobson, Fulton, California

On Friday, March 27, 1993, armed federal marshals, accompanied by a team of U.S. Army Corps of Engineers under authority of a federal search warrant, descended on Jacobson's farm to *investigate claims that cultivation two years ago disrupted vernal pools and endangered plants (a wetlands violation)*. A vernal pool is a depression in the earth which retains water long after winter rains have passed. The environmentalists say that vernal pools are important because they provide a habitat for several kinds of rare and endangered species and therefore it should not be lawful to disrupt a vernal pool via construction or farming. *The environmental socialists have therefore gotten stiff penalties passed for any interference with vernal pools (i.e., fines of up to $5,000 per day; confiscation of property; and federal jail sentences of up to five years).*

The Jacobson saga began when he was told by local fire officials that the weeds growing on his family farm were becoming a hazard and would have to be removed. He checked with several mowing services and found the cost to clear his land would be several thousand dollars. Alternatively he decided to plow-under the weeds so that oats could be planted for the harvest in the coming spring. He used an 8-inch blade, he used no fertilizers, and no insecticides--all he did was plow the soil and plant the seeds *on his own land.*

But now, for the federal crime of farming near a "so-called" vernal pool (never mind that it was on Jacobson's own land), and as an agent from the Army Corps of Engineers said, *"creating significant impact on the hydrology of the soil, including changing how pools are fed by rain and how they drain,"* Jacobson could lose his property, be heavily fined, or go to jail for up to five years.

There are several interesting aspects to the Jacobson case:

1. As in the Berger case above and in Waco, *local or county law enforcement officials were ignored as the Feds moved in.*
2. Jacobson's constitutionally protected rights to do as he wishes with his own private property are being totally ignored.
3. *The enviro-socialists have come up with a whole new vocabulary and body of legalistic environmental laws whereby they can control and/or seize virtually any private property in America and jail any landowners who resist their encroachments* or dictates regarding that property.
4. Jacobson, on advice from his attorney, had resisted for over a year the Feds coming onto his land to conduct a criminal wetlands investigation. The federal agents involved in the raid said that they had decided to raid the Jacobson farm because of his longstanding refusal to cooperate with the authorities. *In other words, the Feds again demonstrated their attitude of*

"we'll get you and make an example out of you if you don't knuckle under and do as we say."

Rusty Hardenburgh, Ohio

In February '93, an FBI SWAT team of over a dozen armed agents swooped down on the Ohio home of Rusty Hardenburgh and confiscated over 100 computers used to power Rusty-N-Edie's BBS (Bulletin Board Service). Hardenburgh had allegedly posted commercial software among its gigabytes of shareware, freeware, GIF images, and other shareware. *No arrests have been made or charges filed, nor are they likely to be.* The informant, in this case, was the Software Publishers Association (SPA), who will undoubtedly get 10 to 25 percent of the proceeds of the 100-plus computers if they are liquidated in a government auction.

The ACLU has argued in defense of Hardenburgh that the seizure of his computers (which effectively put him out of business) is unconstitutional. The FBI argues that their seizure was "evidence gathering." But, as *PC Magazine* (May 11, 1993) said: *"The computers are not evidence of anything. . . . This seizure is harassment, pure and simple."* As *PC Magazine* points out, if this BBS can have its computers confiscated simply because it is "suspected" (not tried, convicted, or found guilty of having pirated software), *"any PC reader 'suspected' of having pirated software can have his PC confiscated."* As in Stalin's Russia, it only takes a tip from an unfriendly neighbor.

[**Note:** *The key factor in this case is that with no criminal or civil charges and no arrest, the computers were seized because of a "tip" and under the "guise" of an investigation. There was no due process, no protection of private property rights, no presumption of innocence until guilt is proven--it is purely and simply Nazi/communist-style plunder of assets by a socialist government now running amuck and out of control.*]

In 1989, Robert Haywood's pharmacy in Royal Oak, Michigan was seized on *"suspicion"* that the pharmacist had allegedly distributed Valium for non-medical purposes. Haywood and his wife have since died and despite the fact that no trial was ever held the business (with its merchandise still on the shelves) and its building, are still held by the government under U.S. drug forfeiture laws. Hundreds more cases of the government's unconstitutionally seizing assets keep surfacing each month.

The present rash of government seizures and forfeitures did not start under Bill Clinton--they actually had their genesis in the Reagan years. *There are several purposes behind the current proliferation of federal, state, and local seizures of private property:*

1. **To raise money** for the law enforcement agencies who, like the "pirates of the Caribbean," divvy up the loot or plunder among themselves or their agencies after a successful raid and seizure.

2. **To nail someone whom they don't like** who resists their regulatory/enforcement efforts, or who protests too loudly about their tactics. There is a growing "get the resistors (or dissidents)" mentality among government agents (or agencies) who will target and pursue a "resistor" with incredible tenacity and vengeance.

3. **High profile publicity**--When the government wants to push a particular program or new form of "people control" (i.e., gun control, child abuse, environmental, anti-alternate medicine legislation) they will seek out a high profile case (often controversial) for a bust, raid, or sting and then try to give it maximum publicity in order to make their point, to energize their program, and gain momentum for further controls.

4. **Intimidate everyone else in that group** into going along with the government in order to avoid similar treatment. *"Operation Intimidation"* can be seen very clearly from the government massacre of almost 100 men, women, and children in Waco. *The message to gun owners and "dangerous religious cults"* (a growing national menace by current liberal definition) *is that if you oppose us, we will crush you.* The intimidation factor is why 100 federal agents were used on day one in Waco, why over 20 agents were used to raid the ranch of the 80-year-old Bergers, and why 10 to 30 gun wielding agents are used routinely against innocent, law-abiding citizens.

5. **People control** is the ultimate goal of these seizures and forfeitures--to prepare the American people to become obedient, passive serfs in the socialist America and New World Order which is being foisted upon us.

Police State Tactics

The heavy-handed tactics of the BATF (and many other federal governmental agencies) seems to know no bounds. On February 5, 1993, the BATF destroyed the home of a Portland, Oregon woman, and terrorized her children for several hours in a case of mistaken identity. Consider the tactics used by the BATF, as described in a March 7, 1993 editorial by Margie Boule in the Portland *Oregonian*, and then realize that these unconstitutional tactics are being used by the BATF, FBI, FDA, EPA, and other federal agencies against thousands of American citizens on a regular basis:

> "*Janice Hart had a car full of kids when she pulled up to her house about 7:30 on the evening of February 5. She'd just returned from grocery shopping. Janice Hart is the mother of two young girls. She's a beautician. She keeps a tidy house.*
>
> "*On this night, a cold midwinter Friday, she had no idea law enforcement officers had been ransacking her house while she was wandering the aisles at Cub Foods, filling her cart with laundry detergent and her daughters' favorite breakfast cereals. She had no idea they wanted to take her to jail.*
>
> "*There was a lot Janice Hart didn't know when she arrived home and saw her front door wide open, uniformed officers streaming in and out. But then, the folks from the federal Bureau of Alcohol, Tobacco, and Firearms had no idea they were raiding the wrong woman's house.*
>
> "*You call it a simple case of mistaken identity. Or you could blame a paid informant who may have been too eager to collect the ATF's financial gratitude for incriminating information. Or you might wonder why these guys don't just go home and let the FBI chase bad guys.*
>
> "*Janice Hart got out of her car. 'I screamed out, What are you doing in my house? Get out of my house!' says Janice. She walked to her side door, holding her house key. But the door was jammed. That's because ATF agents had kicked it in to gain access to the house, and then had nailed it shut.*
>
> "'*Then this officer tells me to identify myself. He says, You know why that door's jammed. You know what's going on. I'm just in a daze. I say, I'm Janice Hart.' Janice says that's when the officer took her by the arm and pulled her inside, saying, 'You're going to jail.'*
>
> "*Janice's daughters, 12 and 4, and a neighborhood friend, 9,*

*heard that part. They got very afraid, very fast. 'I was crying,'
says Nina, Janice's 12-year-old. 'They say, Shut up and get back
in the car. So I put up my knee like to get out, and he shut the door
on my knee.' Nina says an officer searched her mother's purse
then, and the trunk of the car. 'But all there was, was groceries.'*

*''Inside, Janice had trouble recognizing her own home. In the
kitchen, men were shoving dishes to the floor. In Janice's
bedroom they were ripping clothes from hangers and emptying
drawers. <u>I'm screaming, Oh my God, what are you doing to my
house? They told me shut up. They said I could talk later. And
they kept saying, You're going to prison, Janice. The whole
house was totally destroyed.</u>' And it was. Janice has pictures.*

*''After about 15 minutes, the three girls were led inside. All
were crying. 'It was dirty,' remembers Randi, who's 4. 'They
throwed all the stuff on my floor. My church clothes were all
pulled down.'*

*'':Janice's parents came to take the children away. That's
when Janice says the ATF agents took her down to her basement
to be interrogated. Janice is putting in a beauty salon in her
basement. That night, she stood in the basement and started
crying, just like her daughters had cried upstairs.*

*'''There's about eight of them down there, and they're asking
me over and over my name, my Social Security number, my
birthdate. On and on, over and over. And I kept answering over
and over. And I'm saying, What did I do? I don't have anything
to hide. And I don't. I'm 36 years old, and except for a
misdemeanor when I did something stupid when I was 18, I have
a totally clean record. No arrests, no nothing.''*

Janice says she sat in her basement answering questions for over an
hour, before anyone had read her her rights. She says she asked to call an
attorney and the agents refused.

*'''Then they started asking me if I'm Janice Marie Harrell. I say,
No, I'm Janice Marie Hart. Then they show me this warrant they
have. They're looking for a girl Janice Marie Harrell, 130
pounds, with scars on her right elbow, right forearm, nose, right
hand, left eye.*

"'Well, I have no scar on my face. I'm not beat up like that. I'm not a street woman. I'm an everyday type, a working-class mother with two children. This is totally shocking to me. I'm like, I'm not the person you're looking for and they say, You are, and I say, We can go through this for 30 days. I bet I can hold out longer than you, because it's the truth. That's when the main investigator, this George Kim, he says to me, You are good, Janice. You're really a professional.'

"Janice asked about the other Janice, the one they were so sure they were interrogating. What had she done? 'They said she was armed and dangerous, that she sells firearms,' says Janice Hart. 'They said she escaped from jail. They said an informant said I was her, and I was selling crack cocaine out of my kitchen door. I don't sell cocaine.'

"The ATF agents had two warrants: an arrest warrant for Janice Marie Harrell and a warrant to search Janice Hart's home for firearms. They found no guns. They found no Janice Marie Harrell, either.

"'After about an hour I asked to see the picture of the girl,' says Janice. 'I looked at that and I laughed. You couldn't believe they would even mistake me for this girl. We're different as night and day. Anybody could tell you--a blind man could tell you that's not me. I got hazel eyes, my hair is longer. I'm heavier.'

"And then there was the business about the scars. 'They pulled up my sleeves, looking for the scars,' Janice says. 'Of course they weren't there. I say, How do I remove scars? Scars just don't disappear.' That's when he started getting this expression on his face like "I think I messed up." But of course they don't want to admit that to you.'

"Janice says they finally read her her rights, 'They're not just telling me I'm going to jail now,' Janice says. 'They're taking me to jail. I was crying bloody murder. That's not like me.'

"A Portland police officer, working with the ATF, took Janice downtown to be fingerprinted. 'And I want this in the paper,' Janice says. 'The Portland police were very, very nice to me. They treated me like a person.' Which is a lot more than Janice can say for the ATF agents. 'Especially George Kim,' she said. 'He was beyond nasty. I will never forget him as long as I live.'

"It took about 30 seconds for the woman in the fingerprint division to look at Janice Hart's fingerprints and shake her head. 'She said, "You guys picked up the wrong person." Then she turned to me and said, "Baby, you can go home."' Out in the hall, Janice says George Kim approached her. 'He has his head hanging down and he's telling me how sorry he is. I said, I bet you are. That's all I said.'

"One of the Portland police officers gave Janice a ride home, offering to fetch her children on the way. He even broke down the same side door since Janice had not been allowed to take her keys. It took Janice and her husband, from whom she's separated, two days to clear out the mess. Lots of things had to be taken to the dump, broken, torn, bent beyond repair. The ATF dropped off a form so Janice could record the damages.

"I recounted Janice's story for Pete McLouth, the resident agent in charge of one of the local ATF offices. 'What you've just said is correct,' Pete says. 'She wasn't identified as Janice Harrell.' Pete says Janice Harrell was 'lodged' a few days later.

"And why was Janice Hart thought to be Janice Harrell? It seems Janice Harrell uses several aliases, and one is Janice Stewart. Stewart is Janice Hart's married name. 'I can't give you any more details,' Pete said, 'because there's still an active investigation underway on the event that led us to her house that evening.'

"Janice Hart said she hadn't been allowed to call a lawyer, hadn't been read her rights. 'I don't think that's accurate,' Pete McLouth said. He says he doesn't know why Kim might have apologized that night 'other than for the inconvenience of coming downtown to straighten out the identity.'

"Janice Hart has lost a lot of sleep since then. She's had trouble eating. She and Nina are going to see a psychiatrist to help with stress. Randi, the 4-year-old, has been angry at school. Janice had to meet with her teacher. And the neighbors don't seem to like Janice Hart anymore. 'If [the ATF agents] were sincere about being sorry, I think they should come out here and straighten this out with my neighbors,' Janice says.

"Janice has been thinking a lot about something one of the officers said to her that Friday night, right after her fingerprints

*were examined and found to be different than Janice Harrell's.
'He turns to me and says, real quiet, Janice, off the record. Come
Monday you need to get yourself a good attorney.'''*

How does this differ from Nazi Germany, or Communist Russia or
China? It differs, because it is happening in the United States--and on a
regular basis! Note the attitude of the BATF agents during the raid, and even
after the raid when they found out they were mistaken. Note the lack of respect
they showed for their "suspect" or her private property and then remember
their actions in Waco. In what ways do they differ from the Gestapo?

In early March, a homemade bomb was found outside a school in
Sandy, Utah. The 16-year-old son of Sharon Drown was suggested as a
possible suspect. On March 8, 1993, officers of the local police department
and the BATF burst into the Drown home with guns drawn. As the *Salt Lake
Tribune* (March 9, 1993) reported:

> *"Sharon Drown and her daughter were talking Friday morning
> in the bedroom of their Sandy home when they heard someone
> yell 'Police.' The girl ran into the hallway where she was met by
> officers who had their guns drawn. They ordered her not to move.*
>
> *'"I saw three guns pointed at my face,' the girl said. 'They led
> me to the couch and would not let me sit down until they checked
> it. They wouldn't even let me go to the bathroom.'*
>
> *"For the next two hours, officers from the Sandy Police
> Department and BATF searched the bedroom of Ms. Drown's
> 16-year-old son, who was not at home. Investigators collected a
> variety of electrical equipment from the boy's room during the
> search, said the youth's mother.*
>
> *'"They took a battery pack from his Tyco Hovercraft I bought
> him three years ago, a little black alarm that he sets in his
> window to warn him if anyone is coming in, and a circuit board
> that was supposed to be his own private radio station,' she said.*
>
> *"She said her daughter and another son, 17, were trauma-
> tized by the search and likely will need counseling. Her 16-year-
> old son has been released from juvenile detention.*
>
> *"Sgt. Kantor said officers served a 'knock and announce'
> warrant on the Drown home that gives the homeowner time to
> open the door voluntarily. If no one answers, law permits the*

police to enter by breaking down the door.''

''Sgt. Kantor said police do not consider Ms. Drown's son a suspect, but only acted on information that he may know something about the attempted bombing.''

The FDA's War Against Alternative Medicine

There is today in America an unholy alliance between the American Medical Association, large pharmaceutical drug companies, and the Food and Drug Administration. It is well known that very little progress has been made in America in recent decades in the curing of most degenerative diseases such as cancer, muscular dystrophy, multiple sclerosis, Alzheimer's, Parkinsons, and many more, not to mention the host of new killer viruses so rapidly proliferating today. The traditional drug/chemical-based therapies which are the cornerstone of American medicine today are meeting, for the most part, with marginal results at best. The great majority of patients with degenerative diseases are not cured and ultimately die of that disease.

On the other hand, there are a number of alternate therapies which have evolved in America and around the world in recent years which have met with a substantially higher degree of success in treating these degenerative diseases than the more traditional approach. These include some combination of nutritional, vitamin, enzymic, detoxification, homeopathic, chiropractic, oxygenation, bio-magnetic, chelation, and herbal therapies, *essentially based on the detoxification of the body and the building of the immune system so that the body can heal itself. Virtually all of these alternate therapies are lumped together by the AMA and the FDA as quackery that is dangerous to the health of the American people.* (Undoubtedly, some are.)

However, many of these therapies have been used for centuries and are presently used with varying degrees of success in clinics all over the world. This writer personally knows several dozen people who have been treated and healed of a number of the worst degenerative or viral diseases, diagnosed by traditional American medicine as terminal.

But, in spite of almost half of the American public turning to some form of alternate medicine in recent years (according to *Newsweek*, June 7, 1993), *the FDA, backed by the AMA and the large drug companies (who, incidentally, finance most of the medical schools and disease research in America--based, of course, on drug therapies) has launched a war to shut down almost all forms of alternate medicine in America, jail many of its practitioners, and to seize their clinics, records, or in the case of vitamin and supplement manufacturers, their manufacturing facilities.*

The FDA is even going across the border into Mexico with impunity, and (with the Mexican authorities turning their heads the other way) arresting U.S. doctors practicing in Mexican clinics, hauling them across the border, and charging them with medical crimes. Some are being jailed.

On March 12, the FDA, in cooperation with the IRS, DEA, U.S. Customs, and local police, conducted 37 raids across the U.S., including California, Florida, Illinois, Indiana, Michigan, Ohio, and Texas. More than 100 so-called "drugs" (i.e., vitamins and supplements) and either clinics using them, or manufacturers of same, were the targets of armed commando-style assaults conducted in 23 cities.

In addition, there were 23 raids conducted on San Diego homes and businesses including the homes of Lance and Jane Griffin and Dr. and Mrs. Marvin Hutchinson (a biochemist). One eyewitness report of the raid on Dr. Hutchinson's house in Chula Vista was particularly disturbing (According to the American Preventative Medicine Association):

"They broke [Dr. Hutchinson's] door down with a battering ram, arrested his wife who was nursing her baby, handcuffed her, grabbed Marvin, handcuffed him, and would not let either come out to talk with me during the course of the 11-hour raid.

"Similarly, in another eyewitness account, Jane Griffin answered the door and was grabbed by the shoulders by a uniformed San Diego policeman who manhandled her several feet back and, in a split second, while a dozen other agents with guns drawn, demanded that everyone freeze."

As APMA also reported: *"In Livonia, Michigan (a suburb of Detroit), Zerbo's Health Food Store was assaulted by eight FDA agents who bolted for products throughout the store after ordering customers out of the store."* Dozens of different supplements (worth millions of dollars) are being seized from health food stores and clinics across the country while manufacturers such as Ken Scott's Highland Laboratories and Dr. Stephen Levine's Nutricology are being raided and shut down. Alternate health clinics such as Dr. Jonathan Wright's Tacoma Clinic in Tacoma, Washington are being raided, computers and records seized, and their bank accounts frozen, and in some instances the doctors are being jailed or having their licenses revoked.

On June 18, FDA Commissioner David Kessler issued proposed regulations (which will go into effect in 60 days) which will ban 90 percent of the supplements now available in the U.S. by classifying them as drugs (only available through prescription), or as unsafe food additives. Vitamins will be reclassified as prescription drugs or will only be available over the counter in minute quantities; mineral supplements, minerals, and herbs will be reclassified as prescription drugs or banned from sale completely.

It is ironic that the same government which pushes safe sex devices; which sponsors freedom of choice in the killing of unborn babies; which is about to push a new, extremely dangerous abortion pill (RU-486); and is pushing for forced government inoculations of all babies; is, by way of contrast, *also moving to ban all freedom of choice in medicine in America.*

Gun Control as Part of the Coming American Police State

Gun control is a major element of moving America into a socialist police state and the New World Order. That's what Operation Waco and the siege at Ruby Creek (the attack on the Weaver family) were all about--staged, pre-planned gun control operations by the BATF. The American people are being rapidly prepared psychologically to accept gun control.

On March 17, 1993, *USA Today*, the Establishment's primary newspaper for "programming" the public on various issues, carried a front-page headline article entitled "Poll: Owners Favor Gun Laws." This pro-gun control propaganda piece said:

> "*Gun owners are siding with gun control advocates in the push for new restrictions on firearms,* a new USA Today/CNN *poll shows. Fifty-seven percent of gun owners favor stricter gun laws. Gun owners strongly oppose an outright ban on handguns--a move favored by non-gun owners. But otherwise gun owners came down solidly in favor of gun control. . . . Among gun owners: 88 percent support the Brady Bill requiring a 7-day waiting period to buy a handgun; 60 percent favor a total ban on possession of assault weapons* [translated semi-automatic rifles]; *60 percent favor limiting individuals to one gun purchase per month. . . . More than one-third of those polled say they fear gun violence at home and at work, and 70 percent of all Americans want stricter gun laws.*"

Ask any three gun owners you know if they favor more gun control. They will laugh at you! The NRA has said the poll was highly distorted by pro-gun control advocates. The article was part of the Establishment drive for gun control propaganda. They are trying to build the momentum and media hype that there is a groundswell of public sentiment to control guns.

Parallels Between Nazi Gun Control and Proposed U.S. Gun Control Laws

Most thinking people are aware that before the Nazi dictatorship in Germany and the communist dictatorships in Russia, China, Cuba, and Eastern Europe were installed, that they first passed gun control laws and then confiscated handguns, rifles, and shotguns. *What most Americans are not aware of is the incredible parallels between the Nazi gun control laws and the Gun Control Act of 1968 (and those which are now evolving in the U.S.).*

The Nazi Weapons Law (March 18, 1938) is the blueprint for gun control in America in the 1990s. The Nazi gun control laws were actually passed and implemented in stages over an 11-year period, so as to not panic German gun owners. Several aspects of these laws in Germany and in America today are:

1. **Every firearms owner was (and will be) required to get a "firearms owner identity card"**--issued by the federal government, including fingerprints and photographs. For those who say, "It can't happen here!" it should be noted that Massachusetts, Illinois, and New Jersey already have such cards. Nazi-style gun control requires "people control." The excuse for the National Firearms Identity Card is that it will keep criminals from getting firearms--but, of course, it will not! [Note: This *registration of the firearms owner, as well as the firearms,* is exactly what the Nazis did, starting with the 1928 law on Firearms and Ammunition.]

2. **Access to ammunition and reloading components (bullets, gun powder, brass, and especially primers) was (and will be) controlled**--You will need to get a police-issued ammunition/reloading components acquisition permit. The production and sale of primers for civilian use will be halted, and lead could even be banned on environmental grounds. Copper, copper alloys, brass, or steel bullets are now classified as armor-

piercing "cop killer bullets" and so prohibited. Other materials will be added to the banned list. Alternatively, bans on ammunition sales may be imposed for "emergency" reasons, as was done in Los Angeles for two weeks during the "Rodney King riots" in the spring of '92.

3. **Access to firearms will be taxed away**--Firearms, and firearms owners will be heavily taxed, with severe penalties for evading the tax. The tax on firearms may rise to 50 percent or 100 percent and on ammunition to 300, 400, or 500 percent of the retail cost (already proposed by Hillary to pay for her socialized medicine program). The cost of gun permits will be raised from $10 or less in some states today, to $50 to $100 and eventually to thousands of dollars per gun. Those who do not renew their permits will have to surrender their firearms to the government--just as under Nazi law.

4. **The Secretary of the Treasury will redefine the term "sporting purpose" to limit your right to own whole classes of firearms**--The gun controllers are today pushing the concept of limiting firearms to "sporting purpose" which will leave at the whim of government bureaucrats which firearms are suitable for you to own. The concept of "sporting purpose" comes straight from the Nazi gun control laws.

[**Note:** Remember that the Nazis disarmed the German people on a piecemeal basis over a decade or so with measures such as these. *It is happening in the same piecemeal fashion in America today!*]

This writer recently came across an excellent book entitled *Gun Control: Gateway to Tyranny* which analyzes in depth the Nazi Weapons Law of March 18, 1938 and the present parallels between the Nazi and the American gun control laws. It is published by Jews for Preservation of Firearms Ownership (2872 South Wentworth Avenue, Milwaukee, WI 53207--Cost $19.95). *Highly recommended! Just a few of the many parallels are:*

The Nazi Law	The U.S. Gun Control Act of 1968, as Amended
● Presumed that the government and people were hostile to each other,	● Adopted this basic Nazi principle, and so exempted government enti-

so only Nazi Party organizations and government officials were exempted from the 1938 law's restrictions (see Sec. 12, 18, 19);

- Presumed government monopoly ownership of weapons, so private ownership--especially of a firearm--was a privilege granted by the government only to select persons (see Sec. 15);

- Required any private person seeking the privilege of owning firearms to prove him/herself "reliable," without specifying the requirements (see Sec. 15);

- Gave the government unrestricted power to decide what kinds of firearms could, or could not be owned by private persons (see Sec. 25).

ties from the controls which applied to law-abiding citizens (see Sec. 925 (a));

- Tracked the Nazi approach, using federal control over inter-state commerce to convert the constitutionally-guaranteed civil right of the law-abiding person to own firearms into a privilege (see Sec. 922 (a) (3-5));

- Followed the Nazi practice by requiring a purchaser of a firearm from a licensed dealer to declare, under penalty of fine and/or imprisonment, that s/he is not barred under the law from acquiring a firearm (see Sec. 922 (a) (6), Sec. 924 (a) (1));

- Adopted the Nazi approach by introducing the term, "sporting purpose"--not defined in the law or regulations--and authorizing the Secretary of the Treasury to decide what firearms could, or could not be own by private persons (see Sec. 925 (d) (3); (e) (2)).

Preview of Coming Gun Control Initiatives
Just a few of the present federal gun control initiatives include:

- Ban on handgun ownership (Sen. Chaffee [R-RI] will file this bill);
- Ban on buying more than two handguns/month (HR 544, Rep. Torricelli [D-NJ]);
- Ban on ammo clips holding more than 5 (five) rounds (S. 108, Sen. Moynihan [D-NY]);
- Ban on 9mm ammunition (S. 178, Sen. Moynihan [D-NY]);

- Sky-high price for firearms or ammunition due to *a 7,500 percent rise in the fee for federal firearms licenses* (S. 496, Sen. Simon [D-IL]) and a *1,000 percent* tax on 9mm, .25, and .32 ammunition (S. 179, Sen. Moynihan [D-NY]);
- Multiple Handgun Transfer Prohibition Act of 1993, to prohibit the transfer of two or more handguns to one person within a 30-day period (S.376);
- Federal gun registration--dealers forced to close due to sky-high fees must by law send sales records to BATF which can then computerize them; a ban on *private* transfer (between individuals) will enable BATF to know exactly who owns what, and so be able to register and then to confiscate your firearms.

[**Note:** There are presently *thirteen* major gun control bills before the Congress.]

On May 5, Senator John Chaffee (R-RI) announced that he would seek a new law requiring handgun owners, with few exceptions, to surrender their firearms for $25 (or the fair market value of each firearm), as part of the nationwide ban on handgun ownership. He also seeks to prohibit the sale, purchase, transfer, manufacture, possession, transportation, and import or export of all handguns and ammunition.

What to Do

Oppose all forms of gun control by putting pressure on your congressmen, senators, state legislators, etc., via letters, phone calls, etc. *The U.S. Constitution, trial by jury, and firearms ownership are our three major bulwarks against the Establishment-imposed New World Order.*

Every American family should have at least one handgun, one rifle, and one shotgun, as a bare minimum (preferably unregistered) and a thousand rounds of ammunition per weapon. Proficiency in hunting, self-defense, or family protection is also very important. If you are into ammunition reloading, enough components to last for several years (or perhaps a lifetime) should be obtained *now* while they are still legal and available.

In many states or cities firearms can still be bought through newspaper ads, or at gun shows on a very low profile, private, trackless basis. When the Brady Bill passes, such sources will instantly be eliminated. It is not necessary (or perhaps even wise) to keep all of your firearms or ammunition in your house or on your property, considering the government's propensity for house-to-house searches (in some future state of emergency), and the BATF's practice of raiding homes in search of firearms. (If you are concerned about such things, hide them. That is not against the law--not yet, at least.) In a future state of emergency, house-to-house searches for firearms could become commonplace. If diversification in your investment portfolio makes sense, then so does diversification in where you keep your weapons.

The Crime Control Act of 1993 (SB 8)

This legislation, SB 8, may be the most dangerous in American history. Originated by Sen. Orrin Hatch (R-UT), it is being pushed by some leading Senate conservative Republicans who want to be tough on crime and criminals, but who must not have read the bill. *It is not an anti-criminal bill-- it is an anti-political action or political dissident bill which calls for property forfeiture and prison sentences for speeches, writings, and assembly.* Almost any kind of political dissent or demonstration can be defined by this bill as terrorism.

SB 8 redefines and vastly expands the government's search and seizure powers (legalizing formerly illegal government activities) and *eliminates citizens' civil redress in suits against government officials and agents (Title VII, Section 2337). In other words, it would preclude Randy Weaver, the Branch Davidian survivors, or Janice Hart from suing the BATF or FBI officials for destruction of property, life, civil rights, etc. It is legal bulletproofing for federal agents such as the BATF.*

Bill Clinton is rumored to have called Sen. Joe Biden (D-DE) to pressure him to get SB 8 passed. The Establishment desperately wants it in their people control arsenal. It is exactly the kind of legislation which Adolph Hitler used to put the chains on the German people in the 1930s.

Property forfeiture and/or jail for speeches, writings, and assembly--Incorporated were provisions of proposed SB 265 titled "Terrorism Death Penalty Act of 1991" and Sen. Biden's SB 266, "Comprehensive Counter Terrorism Act of 1991." Both bills contain language which can charge law-abiding citizens with being agents or affording support to terrorist organizations.

Consider: the property forfeiture effects on organizations and individuals when speeches, writings, and assemblies mentioned in SB 265 are combined with the forfeiture provisions of Biden's SB 266 now incorporated in the Crime Control Act of 1993: *any individual or organization in the*

United States who had or should have had knowledge that an associate might commit a terrorist act can have their property seized. Written like federal drug forfeiture laws, a citizen who allowed their home or other real property to be used for an assembly would start out guilty, having to prove they did not have knowledge of the unlawful methods of the organization or individuals they allowed to use their property.

Politically active organizations and labor unions are especially vulnerable to the Crime Control Act of 1993 provisions which define bodily acts as "terrorist acts." A fist fight at a demonstration or picket line would qualify. The physical act need not cause bodily harm as its provisions refer to "involving any violent act."

S.8, the Crime Control Act of 1993, forfeiture provisions which seem *aimed at public dissent* are written like RICO laws taking on the added prospect of political property forfeiture. *Broadly written, intent to commit terrorist acts is defined: "appear to be intended (1) to intimidate or coerce a civilian population, (2) to influence the policy of a government by intimidation or coercion."*

It would appear that provisions contained in Senator Biden's proposed SB 266, now included in the Crime Control Act of 1993, target any group of persons which would dare demonstrate for or against any issue. Any picket line which is alleged to have blocked public access could qualify to intimidate or coerce a civilian population. Should violence result for any reason at a public assembly, the property forfeiture provisions of the Crime Control Act of 1993 may be triggered causing forfeiture of attending demonstrators' homes used for meetings, and the vehicles used for transportation to the event. *Demonstrators and/or pickets who left messages on a member's or organization's computer BBS system could cause the forfeiture of the system and all its records.* The fact the system operator had no knowledge of any planned violence will not prevent property forfeiture of assets. Conspiracy is enough: under the provisions of the Crime Control Act of 1993 property forfeiture, arrest, huge fines, and prison sentences can result from *"activities which appear to be intended toward violence." Distributing political action flyers could qualify.*

The Crime Control Act of 1993 when first examined is misleading for it gives the reader the impression that it is after agents of a foreign power wishing to do Americans harm. The "Trojan Horse" in "The Crime Control Acts of 1993": *anyone in the United States committing an undefined violent act or attending an assembly can be charged with terrorism.*

Discovery of witnesses and evidence eliminated--If a defendant under Section 2333 of Title VII, regarding terrorist acts and/or conspiracy, seeks to discover from the Department of Justice the evidence against him, the attorney for the government may object on the grounds that compliance will interfere with a criminal investigation or prosecution of the incident, or a national security operation related to the incident, which is the subject of civil litigation. Example: Government civil forfeiture. Expected: *Defense against government charges may be difficult where citizens have no access to knowing of the alleged evidence against them or the right to cross examine government's secret witnesses.*

Secret witnesses--secret trials: protection of jurors and witnesses in capital cases--Chapter 113B, Section 138 states that the list of veniremen and witnesses need not be furnished to *capital offense defendants* should the court find there to be a preponderance of the evidence that providing the list may jeopardize the life or safety of any person.

Title VII, Section 2337: The Crime Control Act of 1993--*eliminates civil suits* against U.S. and foreign governments by persons injured by government agents while in pursuit of preventing terrorist acts.

Title VII, Section 711: Sentencing guidelines increased for terrorist crimes--The United States Sentencing Commission shall have the power to provide an increase in the base offense level for any felony committed in the United States that involves or is intended to promote international terrorism. *Participation by political activists in lawful speeches, writings, and public assemblies may be used as evidence by government to show that a political participant was aware of the unlawful methods of the individual or organization they are alleged to have afforded support.*

One person's violent act at an assembly may be enough for the government to allege the assembly *appears to be intended toward violence or activities which could intimidate or coerce a civilian population.*

Under current drug forfeiture laws--innocent citizens have been implicated by informants who will often testify to anything to mitigate their own arrest. This has resulted in innocent citizens being arrested and killed by drug agents; forfeiture of their property; and financial ruination. Under proposed provisions of the Crime Control Act of 1993 special breaks are afforded informants, even against the death penalty. Government will have no difficulty ''creating informants'' to cause the incarceration of any citizen considered a threat to one's political agenda.

Disproportionate zero tolerance laws have served as precedents

for expanding forfeiture--*Since 1984, forfeiture laws have been operating on the erroneous contention that property can possess intent to commit crime.* Innocent owners can have their property seized prior to trial on mere suspicion, starting out guilty, the owner having to prove they did not have reason to know that their property was being used to facilitate a forfeitable offense. Government need only show the property owner was negligent in making their property available for illegal drug activity to cause its forfeiture.

The forfeiture scam--*tenants arrested on real property when offered a sentencing deal by a prosecutor or immunity from further prosecution, often reply in testimony, "that had the real property owner been vigilant, he or she could have discovered drug activity taking place on their property."* Government has used against real property owners in civil forfeiture actions the fact that the property owner had reported to police that a tenant was dealing drugs to show the owner had prior knowledge of the activity at their property. Elderly citizens afraid to face machine guns and other threats by drug dealers are especially vulnerable to having their homes and rental property seized. Elderly property owners are easy prey for police forfeiture squads. (See the case of Paul and Rosie Berger.)

The Crime Control Act of 1993--will allow government to use against its citizens, illegally seized evidence. Searches, wire taps, and seizures that result in obtaining evidence from an invalid warrant but *was carried out in reasonable reliance on a warrant issued by a detached and neutral magistrate found to be invalid based on misleading information or reckless disregard of the truth,* may in many instances override constitutional Fourth Amendment protection against illegal search and seizure.

S.8, The Crime Control Act of 1993--amends the "exclusionary rule" to add Section 3509 Admissibility of Evidence Obtained by Search or Seizure (a) Evidence Obtained by Objectively Reasonable Search or Seizure; (b) Evidence Not Excludable by Statute or Rule; *sets the groundwork for forfeiture squads to at random invade innocent owner's homes and businesses with a minimum of probable cause.* Government need only assert that *"a search and seizure was carried out in circumstances justifying an objectively reasonable belief that it was in conformity with the Fourth Amendment."*

Informants--Now being paid by government up to 25 percent of net proceeds realized from forfeited assets in drug related seizures could earn similar amounts causing forfeiture of citizen's homes they allege to have been used by an owner for discussion of attending assemblies which the informant believed *"appeared to be intended toward violence or to intimidate or coerce a civilian population."*

The Crime Control Act of 1993--Informants and law enforcement agencies addressing prevention of terrorist acts are to be funded by forfeiture and fines collected from terrorists and/or persons alleged to have afforded terrorist material support. *Will citizens exercising their constitutional right to free expression and association be targeted by government agents who know their jobs are dependent on property seizures, fines, and arrests?*

What to Do

There is next to *no* grass roots opposition to the Crime Control Act of 1993. Very few people, groups, editorials, or politicians are even talking about it. *It is imperative that grass roots opposition to this legislation be mounted immediately.* Contact your senators and congressmen and express your strong opposition immediately. *Pro-Constitution, pro-life, pro-traditional values editorialists, newsletters, and other publications need to publicize this Nazi-style people control, dissent-stifling legislation immediately!* It would seem that next to no one in the Congress (except its Establishment drafters) has read this nightmarish legislation which totally violates our First Amendment rights to free speech, writing, assembly, and demonstrations. Bill Clinton seems to desperately want it passed. It must be stopped! As Edmund Burke said, *"All that's necessary for evil to triumph is that good men do nothing."*

Toward a National and International Police Force

The national police force which Bill Clinton and Al Gore talked about in their book, *Putting People First,* is presently being assembled. The immediate goal is 100,000 federal agents, but if agents of the BATF, FBI, DEA, FDA, EPA, and a dozen other agencies are included, the total number will reach 200-300,000 within two or three years.

The National Guard will figure very prominently in the national police force (as will the U.S. military). General Colin Powell, head of the Joint Chiefs of Staff, said during the week of February 8 that *"the government plans to unify all the various states' National Guards under one command to deal with national emergencies and disasters."* [**Note:** It is significant that the massacre of the Branch Davidians in Waco was a joint venture between the FBI, BATF, and the U.S. military.]

Remember that the National Guard was federalized and brought in to quell the Los Angeles riots in April/May '92. A National Guard officer from Kentucky was recently brought to Los Angeles to help in planning for future riot control in that city. For several years National Guard troops have been training to do house-to-house searches for firearms and drugs.

In April, the Nevada state legislature passed legislation authorizing the state to enter into an agreement to move its National Guard troops around the country to other states to participate in "drug interdiction and *other operations.*" As the *Las Vegas Review-Journal* wrote in an editorial on April 11, 1993:

> *"Our form of government was founded on the principle that authority should be dispersed as widely as possible, <u>on theory that local officials are less likely to resort to tyranny than some distant bureaucrat.</u>*
>
> *"By the same token, our national guardsmen came from our own states on the perfectly sensible theory that an off-duty garage mechanic from Tonopah is less likely to shoot an old lady at a police barricade in Las Vegas, than is some mercenary from Alabama. . . . <u>Do Nevadans really want to give federal storm troopers the power to dispatch our guardsmen to far-off places to shoot people for using drugs or whatever? Not on your life!</u>"*

Jack McLamb, a former Arizona police officer and the editor of the *Aid and Abet* newsletter has written:

> *"The ultimate goal of the government bureaucrats is creation of a world government, the laws or rules of which would be enforced by a national police force. . . . The idea of a national police force originated with LEAA, the Federal Law Enforcement Assistance Administration. In 1969 Charles Rogovin of LEAA warned police chiefs that a national police force might be needed.*
>
> *"And Patrick Murphy, president of the Police Foundation, created by the Ford Foundation in 1970, noted: 'I have no fear of a national police force. Crime control is not working, and our 40,000 police departments are not sacred. The danger is insignificant. The greater danger is that crime may worsen, that the*

states will refuse to coordinate and the federal government will not require them to. In fact, the government is now loosening the strings, and the states are doing next to nothing. Policing is not effective. We worship local government and home rule in this country--I like it, too--but the problem must be solved by a higher level of government, like welfare."

McLamb explains how the federal government has been moving to take over local law enforcement agencies all across America, just as they did the educational system, starting some three decades ago.

"The government long since decided to seize control from the top, claiming as usual that they are doing just the opposite, that all they are doing is helping the police. So they do everything they can to create a crime wave. And at the same time they do everything they can to prevent the local police from stopping it. Then they announce that the local police need their help--to fight crime--and they begin by handing them federal aid, <u>knowing that whatever the government finances, it controls.</u> Of course, they tell the police chiefs that there are no strings attached. That is what the dope pusher tells the kids on the playground. But gradually, like the pusher, they begin to impose rules. They know that, before the chiefs and the people realize it, they will be in control. <u>Once corrupt politicians 'control' law enforcement officers, the rights of common citizens will be meaningless.</u>"

[**Note:** In police and county sheriff's departments all across the country, officers are being trained (programmed) for the national police force, for the New World Order, and to think of the public as the opposition, or the "other side." Older officers who resist this national police force programming are either being forced out or are becoming disgusted and quitting.]

What Is the Multi-Jurisdictional Task Force?

A great deal of rumors and unconfirmed information are surfacing regarding the Multi-Jurisdictional Task Force, but *at this time it is hard to confirm all of the information in the following paragraph.* This information is coming from so many sources that this writer felt it needed to be shared. But at this time it is *not* confirmed.

A major part of the new national police force is said to be the *Multi-Jurisdictional Task Force* (MJTF)--made up of military personnel; agents from various government agencies (i.e., BATF, FBI, IRS, EPA, CIA, DEA, federal marshals, etc.); federalized National Guard troops; some federalized local and state police; and conceivably federalized street gangs to be used for house-to-house searches in cities such as Los Angeles, Chicago, and New York. The MJTF police mission is said to be house-to-house searches, and seizure of property and firearms; separation and categorization of men, women, and children as prisoners in large numbers; transfer to, and operation of the 43 "alleged" federal detention camps. MJTF police are said to be seen frequently around the U.S. now in black uniforms and often flying black surveillance helicopters. [**Note:** Information on the MJTF police is still very sketchy, but recent events in Waco give its existence some credence.]

In April, Bill Clinton announced that he plans a military/police merger for the U.S. Presented as civilian control of the military, in practice it gives the military responsibility and training for civil domestic duties. Along this line, the following article from the Stockton (California) *Register* (March 4, 1993) entitled "Marines Practice Storming Stockton" is worth pondering:

> *"If Marine helicopters start buzzing your house today or to-night, don't be alarmed. It's only a drill. The 13th Marine Expeditionary Unit from Oceanside will conduct 'urban environment training.'. . .*
>
> *"'People will not notice the training on the ground because we travel to and from sites in civilian clothes,' said Marine Chief Warrant Officer Hartman Slate, a spokesman for the trainers. 'What they will see is the helicopters,' Slate said. The aircraft will include Cobra attack helicopters and the cargo and troop transport Super Stallion, 'the free world's largest helicopter.'*
>
> *"'At night, as they fly at the lowest point, about 20 stories high, you may hear the flying machines but not see them because they will be flying with their lights off and using night-vision goggles,' said Marine Sgt. Dave Hiersekorn."*

Since communism has been declared dead, *although it isn't*, the government has to find ways to keep the U.S. military "busy and challenged." Participation in domestic crowd/dissident/gun control seems to be right down their alley.

Chapter Three

The Waco Massacre:
Trial by Fire
(A Case Study in Police State Tactics in America)

On Monday, April 19, 1993 the U.S. government, in an act of mass murder unrivaled in U.S. history, burned 86 people, including 24 children, to death in the Branch Davidian compound in Waco, Texas--climaxing a 51-day siege launched by the Bureau of Alcohol, Tobacco, and Firearms (BATF), on February 28, 1993. As editorialist Charley Reese recently wrote:

> *"When you start with an 'allegation' that a gun control law has been violated, and you end up with nearly 100 people, including 25 children, killed, and millions of taxpayers dollars down the drain, that's bad law enforcement no matter how you slice it."*

On February 28, the U.S. government launched an assault with 100 warriors and large amounts of military equipment against the Branch Davidian commune, their church, and their home near Waco, Texas. The original attack left four BATF agents dead and 16 wounded, and somewhere between 5 and 10 Branch Davidians dead. The attack had been planned for nearly a year, using an almost identical replica compound in Arkansas built for training by the BATF. Photographs taken by aircraft provided the exact dimensions of all structures, as well as the locations of the windows and doors.

The BATF botched the original raid in every way possible, maintaining that they were simply trying to serve a search warrant to look for illegal weapons inside the compound. There seems a strong possibility that at least some of the BATF agents were killed or wounded by "friendly" fire from their own men, or from the helicopter gunships overhead. Several unarmed Branch Davidians not in the compound, but on or near the grounds, were shot and killed by BATF snipers at the time of the raid (or that evening). Military helicopters shot at the compound from above and killed a young girl sitting on her bed nursing her baby.

The final raid involved the FBI (who took over after the BATF botched the operation) and the U.S. Marines attacking the compound with tanks, punching holes in the walls, pumping in a battlefield chemical warfare agent (CS gas) for six hours, and igniting fires that killed all 86 inhabitants (i.e., 62 adults and 24 children, including 17 under 10 years of age). As the *Los Angeles Times* wrote: *"Almost as many Americans died in the two assaults as died in the entire Gulf War."* In the aftermath of the massacre, President Clinton, Attorney General Janet Reno, and officials of the FBI defended their action, claiming the Branch Davidians set fire to their own compound, committing a massive, pre-planned suicide.

Koresh and his followers held no hostages, had committed no violent crimes, were not threatening to kill or harm anyone. They were minding their own business on their own property. Everyone in the compound was there of their own free will. Texas social workers had been in the compound and found no indication that any outsider who visited the compound would be in any danger. One of the children living in the compound told her father, according to him, that "it was a joy to live there."

A massive cover-up by the Clintonistas, the FBI, the BATF, and the Establishment-controlled media has pacified the great majority of the American public in spite of the worst massacre of men, women, and children by our government in U.S. history. President Clinton and the Establishment's message in the aftermath was clear: Let this be a warning to religious misfits, dissidents, gun regulations violators, Constitutionalists, and traditionalists: Get in our way, oppose us, or thumb your nose at us and we will destroy you.

What a horror to watch men, women, and children burned to death for no other crime than resisting the omnipotent state. *It is a chilling example of the police state that is emerging in America with ominous parallels to Nazi Germany, which "coincidentally" massacred hundreds of Jews in the Warsaw ghetto exactly 50 years earlier on April 19, 1943. Gun control, people control, persecution of religious minorities, and incredible ruthlessness and wickedness were all part of the Third Reich in Germany and are part of the Fourth Reich emerging in America today.*

The Branch Davidians were not the first group the BATF has attacked for "alleged" gun control violations. *Last year alone, the BATF raided over 2,000 homes or businesses with a number of innocent victims killed, and tens of millions in assets seized and hundreds of Americans*

jailed, in their quest for the Holy Grail called gun control.
As syndicated columnist Paul Craig Roberts noted:

"The tragedy near Waco happened precisely because of federal laws regulating gun ownership. The Branch Davidians hadn't assaulted anyone. They lived peacefully in the community. Except for federal gun laws they would all still be alive. It is the liberal premise that gun ownership is evil, should be illegal, or at least heavily regulated, and that has created an atmosphere in which the BATF like an unthinking bully, can run roughshod over Americans' rights, due process, and freedom."

It is obvious that the government wanted a highly publicized "victory" over gun owners and "religious nuts," and thanks to the whitewashing and cover-up by the Administration and the media, the American people have by-and-large slept through the most unspeakable slaughter of innocents in U.S. history. In spite of all the mess-ups, the government has its victory, *gun owners and religious groups across America now live in fear of similar treatment at the hands of Clinton's Gestapo, and the momentum toward gun control, toward persecution of Christians and other minority religious groups, traditionalists, and Constitutionalists, and towards a socialist America and the New World Order continues to accelerate.*

The Final Attack: The Fiery Holocaust

At 6:30 a.m., Monday, April 19, government tanks began ramming and punching holes in the Mt. Carmel compound and a Special Operations team from Quantico, Virginia began pumping CS gas into the gaping holes in the buildings. Within hours 86 people were dead, victims of a raging inferno that may well have been started by the military tanks puncturing a propane tank and overturning lanterns used by the Branch Davidians for light and heat, after federal officers cut off the power to the compound some 50 days before.

The Davidian compound was a tinderbox constructed of used lumber, plywood, and sheetrock tacked together with tar paper. Its floors were littered with combustibles, including bales of hay and kerosene, gasoline, and propane on which the Branch Davidians were largely dependent after electricity was cut off by the government. The potential for fire was obvious from the start and well understood by the government.

If the inhabitants of Mt. Carmel had been dangerous terrorists, drug dealers, or enemies on the battlefield, the government attack could not have been more brutal. After the initial attack (February 28, 1993) former McClennon County Texas District Attorney Vic Feazell blamed the BATF for the deadly confrontation, accusing them of "a vulgar display of power."

In 1987, Feazell helped lead an investigation of the Davidians in which they were completely exonerated from any illegal activity. *"We treated them like human beings rather than stormtrooping the place."*

Likewise, Jack Harwell, the McClennon County sheriff, called Koresh on the telephone and informed him of the charges, and asked him to turn himself in, along with six others and to surrender their weapons. When deputies arrived at the church grounds, Koresh and the other Davidians peacefully complied. Feazell said of the Davidians,

> *"They're protective of what's theirs. They're protective of their land. They view their land as Muslims to Mecca and Jews view Jerusalem. . . . If they'd (the BATF) called and talked to them, the Davidians would've given them what they wanted."*

Feazell's view of the BATF blundering has been seconded by anti-terrorist expert Col. Charlie Beckwith, the founder of the U.S. Army's Delta Force Commando unit. He has told reporters the BATF raid was an "embarrassment." Beckwith faulted the plan implemented by the BATF, saying the intelligence behind it was responsible for the disaster.

Subsequent to the first BATF attack Feazell predicted that the government would kill all the Davidians, and after the massacre he said that *they intended to kill these people from the beginning to cover the tracks of their own crimes they committed by raiding the compound to begin with.*

After the original public relations disaster on February 28, the government strategy seems to have evolved over the next 51 days as follows:

1. Through a massive media discrediting the Davidians through the "party line" press over several weeks;
2. By slowly preparing the public to believe that all of the people remaining in the compound were under the total control of an unpredictable psychopath, and to expect a mass suicide, yet saying that there was no reason for them to believe that Koresh

would carry out a mass suicide;

3. To cloak their act in righteousness (as tyranny always does) by saying their efforts on Monday were to force the people out using non-lethal CS gas "for the sake of the children."

Using CS Gas on Children

President Clinton, Janet Reno, and their FBI/BATF employees have described CS gas as "a harmless tear gas, an irritant, designed to cause the mothers to grab their children and run out of the building." No one in the police or military who has ever used CS gas believes this. CS gas (O-chlorobenzylidene malonitrite) has been *banned as a chemical warfare battlefield agent by the Chemical Weapons Convention signed in Paris in January by the U.S. and 130 other nations.* Used during the Vietnam War to flush Vietcong from hidden tunnels, *the gas causes dizziness, disorientation, shortness of breath, chest tightness, nausea, burning of the skin, intense tearing, temporary blindness, coughing, and vomiting--in short it is designed to blind and disable (very different from "relatively harmless"). CS gas is a battlefield incapacitating gas!*

On March 10, *The Houston Chronicle* reported that former Houston police SWAT commander Lt. Jim Gunn said that *"CS gas can get into a child's lungs and cause congestion and kill them."* Benjamin C. Garrett, executive director of the Chemical and Biological Arms Control Institute in Alexandria, Virginia, said in the *Washington Times* (April 23, 1993) that *"the CS would have most harshly affected the children in the compound. The reaction would have intensified for the children since the smaller you are, the sooner you would feel response."* It is important to note that the children did not have gas masks (they were too small to wear them).

Beth Stephens, a lawyer with the Center for Constitutional Rights, a public interest law firm based in New York, said *"tests have documented at least 80 deaths caused by exposure to CS gas. Tests have found that CS is a toxic substance which is highly dangerous to people who inhale its fumes, particularly when in confined areas."* CS was pumped into the Mt. Carmel compound (an enclosed area) for *six hours* before the facility caught fire and burned to the ground.

The *Washington Times* (March 22, 1993) wrote:

"The powerful chemical the FBI used at the Branch Davidian compound would have turned the cult children's last moments

into a final hell,' chemical experts said yesterday. 'It would have panicked the children whose eyes would have involuntarily shut. Their throats and lungs would have been burning. They would have been coughing wildly,' said Benjamin Garrett. 'Eventually they would have been vomiting in a final hell.'''

Thomas C. Swearengen, in his authoritative reference work, *Tear Gas Munitions*, states:

> *"In <u>outdoor</u> situations where it is desired to drive a mob from an area, the use of CS may hamper the movement of the rioters <u>because of the rapid onslaught of immobilization symptoms.</u> In <u>indoor</u> situations, a victim could be immobilized and could possibly receive a lethal dose through his own helplessness."*

Amnesty International calls CS

> *". . . particularly dangerous when used in <u>massive quantities</u> in heavily built up and populous areas . . . or when launched into homes or other buildings."*

This writer has talked to a half dozen special forces, military, and police personnel who all agree that CS is a highly toxic battlefield immobilization gas. "Bo" Gritz told this writer that, *"CS gas is not just an irritant; it is designed to knock you down and makes you incapable of any practical functions." That our government would use it on women and children is cruel, inhuman, and unspeakably evil, and is the kind of thing the Nazis and communists would have relished.*

Isn't it ironic that Clinton and company are pushing criminal child abuse laws for spanking children, refusing to get forced government inoculations, etc., but then helped perpetrate this crime (the greatest example of government child abuse in U.S. history) on 24 innocent children. Ignore what they say, but watch what they do!

CS Gas Is Highly Flammable in Enclosed Areas

U.S. Army Special Forces retired Lt. Col. "Bo" Gritz has said that the use of CS gas in an enclosed space set the stage for a total inferno. When the buildings exploded into flames, it was like they were filled with natural gas. Flames exploded everywhere almost all at once. Gritz has said on several national radio talk shows (including one with this writer) that

> ". . . the dispersant used in CS gas, known in military assault circles as 'CAP,' is a highly flammable dust initiator. Just a small spark would cause CS gas to explode into an uncontrollable and engulfing fire."

CS gas, dispersed in a fine white particulant (powder) called CAP is therefore highly flammable and explosive. It acts like dust in a grain elevator that can be ignited into a conflagration by just one spark. This writer has talked to a half dozen active duty or retired military personnel, police, and government agents who have had hands on experience with CS gas. All acknowledged that it is highly flammable and explosive in an enclosed area and that that is common knowledge in the military and the police.

If that is true (and it is!) then the FBI and the Clinton people must have known that by pumping the CS gas into the enclosed compound, that they were signing the Branch Davidians' collective death warrant. Therefore, the strong possibility needs to be considered that the Waco conflagration was not an accident, that it wasn't mass suicide, but premeditated, cold-blooded murder of 86 people--in order to burn up the evidence of the BATF's illegal/unconstitutional attack on the compound on February 28--just as former McClennon County District Attorney Vic Feazell suggested.

One survivor said that:

> ". . . the black smoke was so thick that within seconds he couldn't see where he was. People were trapped. The building was falling down. The damn tanks had just destroyed the structure and nobody knew where they were because the ceiling had just fallen in. Everyone was disoriented and blinded by the [CS] gas."

Isn't it incredible! The American government has agreed not to use CS gas against Iraqi (or any other) enemy soldiers, but used it against helpless women and children. What has our government come to? And most Americans don't even see anything wrong with their actions!

Was the Waco Holocaust a Mass Suicide?
All of the survivors said that there was no plan for a mass suicide or even individual suicides. The Branch Davidian religion (an offshoot of

Seventh Day Adventism and totally different from that of Jim Jones) forbade and taught against suicide. It should also be remembered that no one commits suicide (except for a few Monks during the Vietnam War) by burning themselves. *There has never been a mass suicide by burning.*

The one thing that all family members have repeated time and again is that no one in the group would have ever committed suicide. Koresh was planning to write a book about the siege. Steve Schneider asked his attorney if he should get his hair cut before he came out of the compound or in jail. There were many indications that these two Branch Davidian leaders and other members were very future oriented and not contemplating suicide.

And yet, Clinton, Reno, and the FBI justified their attack on the compound by saying that they feared a mass suicide. Then, after the gas ignited a raging inferno that killed the 86, they said, "See, we told you we feared a mass suicide." Could this have been a very Machiavellian government strategy to get rid of the incriminating evidence of their botched, unconstitutional February 28 raid by burning all the evidence and embarrassing court testimony, and calling it mass suicide?

Koresh was found with a bullet hole in his *forehead*. Police friends tell this writer that people don't commit suicide by shooting themselves in the forehead. Koresh's first lieutenant, Steve Schneider, was found with a bullet hold in the *back* of his head. People don't commit suicide by shooting themselves in the back of the head. Were the bullets fired later by government agents to make it look like suicide? We will never know!

Government Justification of the Massacre:
Operation Cover Their Backsides

President Clinton's press conference and damage control--President Clinton gave a Rose Garden press conference on April 20, 1993 in which he defended the actions of Reno, the FBI, and the BATF in Waco. The lies and distortions which Clinton told in this press conference were incredible:

1. *"The Branch Davidians had illegally stockpiled weapons and ammunition."* That was only suspected, but never proven. Shouldn't the government have proven that before they killed almost 100 people? Is it now lawful to kill people during investigations of wrongdoing? Lawful or not, it is now commonplace in America!

2. Koresh *"placed innocent children at risk."* There was no risk

until the government attacked the compound. Wasn't it the government that put the innocent children at risk?

3. *"The Bureau's efforts were ultimately unavailing because the individual with whom they were dealing, David Koresh, was dangerous, irrational, and probably insane."* None of the townspeople who knew Koresh observed this, nor did the former district attorney of McClennon County, nor the sheriff's deputies who knew him. He did have strange religious views, but most of the townspeople who knew him liked him.

4. Clinton said the April 19 FBI attack on the Branch Davidians was *"an effort to protect the young hostages."* The government didn't protect them, they killed them. And, the children were *not* hostages. They were there of their own free will. *The Waco siege was never a hostage crisis.*

5. Clinton said, *"The [FBI] plan included a decision to withhold the use of ammunition, even in the face of fire, and instead use tear gas that would not cause permanent damage."* No one knows who fired at who during the final siege, because the press were kept two miles away, unless one wants to accept Clinton's word, and the government *did not* use tear gas--it was highly lethal, flammable CS gas.

6. Clinton said, *"Mr. Koresh's response to the demand for his surrender by federal agents was to destroy himself and murder the children who were his captives. . . . He killed those he controlled."* There is no evidence that Koresh murdered any children; it is open to question whether at the last moment he shot himself; and the children (according to local townspeople and Texas social workers) were *not* captives.

7. Clinton said, *"I hope very much that others who will be tempted to join cults and to become involved with people like David Koresh will be deterred by the horrible scenes they have seen over the last seven weeks."* Is this *a not-so-veiled threat* that if you belong to an unpopular, misfit, non-main-stream religious group, the same thing could happen to you? *The intimidation value from the Waco inferno for the government against small religious groups, conservative, patriotic, pro-life, or non-mainstream groups is incredible.*

8. When asked by a reporter, "Why now?" Clinton replied,

"There was a limit to how long the federal authorities could maintain with their limited resources the quality and intensity of coverage by experts there. They might be needed in other parts of the country." Limited resources? This is the government which is giving billions of dollars to Russia in aid and requesting billions more for 1,001 boondoggles. And as far as spreading the "experts" too thin, there were only a few hundred troops and agents there. The government has tens of thousands of federal agents and allegedly over a million military personnel.

9. Clinton said, *"The danger of them [the Branch Davidians] doing something to themselves or to others was likely to increase, not decrease, with the passage of time."* Quite to the contrary, as time went by, the likelihood that they would come out increased, according to experts who have dealt with many of these types of crises.

10. Clinton said, *"They [the FBI] had reason to believe that the children inside the compound were being abused significantly, as well as being forced to live in unsanitary and unsafe conditions."* There was no evidence of child abuse according to several Texas social workers who had visited the compound. However, the gassing and burning of the children by the Clintonistas does seem to qualify as child abuse. And if the conditions were unsanitary and unsafe in the compound it was because the government had turned off the water, heat, and electricity 50 days earlier. Government gunfire into the building might also qualify as an "unsafe condition."

11. Clinton said, *"I was frankly surprised to see that anyone would suggest that the attorney general should resign because some religious fanatics murdered themselves."* But what if the attorney general and her subordinates murdered these people? Will *your* religious group be the next one to be labeled by Mr. Clinton or Ms. Reno as "dangerous religious fanatics"?

12. Clinton said, *"There is unfortunately a rise in this sort of fanaticism all over the world. And we may have to confront it again."* Is that a veiled threat against other religious non-conformist groups?

Jack Wheeler, a contributing editor to the *Strategic Investment Newsletter*, summed it up quite well:

"Let me state things clearly. It is one thing to be laughably incompetent, quite another to be murderously incompetent. I think the president should be impeached and the attorney general indicted for murder. To hear how over 20 children endured a nightmare of torture by CS poison gas, and then see the attorney general praised in Congress and hear the president ruthlessly dismiss their deaths in a tone of voice as devoid of humanity as Lenin's has for the first time in my life made me ashamed of being an American."

The Child Abuse Accusation

"Child abuse" is the new buzz phrase and headline grabber by the Clintonistas and their political left in America, and *by their definition* can include spanking your children; failure to get your children mandatory government inoculations; failure to teach your children about alternate lifestyles; and eventually home schooling may be included.

The Clinton Administration has tried to justify their Waco massacre by accusing the Branch Davidians of being child abusers. (*It is very important Constitutionally to note that child abuse does not fall under the authority of the federal government.*) President Clinton, Janet Reno, and other officials, through their spokesman George Stephanopoulos, said on April 21, 1993: *". . . there is absolutely no question that there's overwhelming evidence of child abuse in the Waco compound."* George Stephanopoulos said: *"The children were being abused, even to the instruction on how to clamp down on cyanide pills"* The FBI has conceded that there was no truth to this claim by Stephanopoulos.

Janet Reno claimed on April 19 that it was concern for the children that had first brought federal attention to the Davidians, that "suspected" sexual abuse of children was a basis for the original raid, and that the decision to punch holes in the compound and insert *"chemical irritants"* was based in part on "information that *informants were being slapped around and beaten." She subsequently admitted, though, that "we can't prove child abuse in terms of a criminal case."*

The facts seem to vary from the Clintonista version. *The Texas child welfare department, which had visited Mt. Carmel several times, said that they found no evidence of child abuse at the compound and they interro-*

gated children and mothers and other adults extensively. Dr. Bruce Perry, the psychiatrist heading the team treating the 21 children who left the compound, said after intensive psychological as well as physical examinations that *"none of the 21 children had been sexually abused or molested."*

The Texas Department of Human Services had on three occasions extensively investigated the Branch Davidians regarding allegations of child abuse at the compound, interviewing both children and adults, and found no signs of physical or sexual abuse. Janice Caldwell, the executive director of the Texas Department of Protective and Regulatory Services, told reporters on March 5: *"They [the 21 children] are in remarkably good shape considering what they have been through. No signs of physical abuse have been found."* Social worker Joyce Sparks said, according to the *Houston Post*, that "the children *were remarkably well-educated and they're fascinated by books."*

The Government Cover-up:
Operation Damage Control (or White Wash)

The U.S. government has refined the art of political cover-up to a science. They have had practice:

1. **The POW/MIA Cover-up** after World War II, Korea, and Vietnam whereby thousands of American POWs and servicemen were left in the hands of the communists;
2. **The Kennedy Assassinations (John and Bobby) Cover-up** which is now in its 31st year;
3. **The Watergate Cover-up** which ultimately backfired on Nixon and Company;
4. **The AIDS Cover-up** presently being perpetrated by the government (and particularly the CDC) to hide the extent and magnitude of the AIDS crisis; and
5. **The Waco Massacre**.

Burning and Bulldozing the Evidence

The BATF (and other government agencies) love to burn, bulldoze, or cremate the evidence. In the Weaver case, the government tried to burn out the Weaver cabin by dumping fuel on the cabin via helicopter and only an alert reporter waving a camera in the air saved the surviving Weavers from the same fate as the Branch Davidians. Shortly after Randy Weaver, Kevin

Harris, and the three Weaver girls came out of the cabin, the BATF and FBI grabbed the bodies of Vicki and Sam Weaver and had them cremated. Therefore, no trial evidence from autopsies. (Sam Weaver, age 14, was shot several times in the back by the marshals, Vicki in the head by an FBI sniper).

When Congressman John Ashbrook (R-OH), who was investigating potentially illegal Rockefeller bank dealings with Russia, died suddenly of massive stomach bleeding over a decade ago, his wife (under pressure from the government) had his body quickly cremated--with no autopsy. Ashbrook's death had all the symptoms of a poisoning. When Gordon Kahl was killed in Arkansas by government agents in 1983, the cabin in which he was killed was burnt to the ground and Kahl's body and all evidence at the crime scene was burned up. (The FBI controlled the crime scene from beginning to end.)

In Waco, on April 19, crucial physical evidence and key witnesses were consumed by fire. Then, on May 12, FBI officials, citing the fear that someone might fall in the bunker (though the entire site was fenced and guarded), and a need to fill holes and cover trash and raw sewage for safety and health reasons, *rolled bulldozers across the burned out compound completely obliterating any remaining evidence.*

The So-Called "Independent" Arson Team
Had Close Ties With the BATF

The Clintonistas, immediately after the fire, suggested an "independent" investigation of the burned out Branch Davidian compound site and confirmation of the "truth." That "independent" investigator, who claimed the fire had been set by the Davidians (based, he said, on infrared photos taken from a helicopter) was revealed on *ABC Nightline* to be a former BATF employee and long time contractor for the FBI, *whose wife is personal secretary to the head of the Houston BATF*--where the whole raid was planned. *The FBI controlled the crime scene for three weeks following the holocaust, letting no Texas Rangers, local police, or truly independent arson investigators in, and then bulldozed the entire site on May 12.*

The Justice Department Will Not Investigate
the Decisions for the Final Assault

Although Bill Clinton promised a "vigorous and thorough" investigation of the handling of the entire Waco affair, *on May 15 the Justice Department said it would not investigate the decision making process associated with the final assault.* (This is like saying in a murder case we will

not investigate who pulled the trigger or who gave the order to pull the trigger.)
As the *New York Times* (May 16, 1993) said:

> *"Clinton officials said that since Ms. Reno has been widely supported in Congress, and since polls show that the majority of Americans supported her decision to use tear gas, and blame the cult members themselves for the final deadly fire, department officials concluded that nothing could be gained by looking more closely at her order to carry out the assault."*

Lies the Government Told During and After Operation Waco

"Governments are constituted to lie to the greatest number of people the greater part of the time" (Machiavelli, in *The Prince*)

BATF, FBI, and Clinton Administration officials have consistently lied and contradicted themselves since the siege of Mt. Carmel began. Just a few of a growing list of the lies include:

1. The media was told the day before the raid (February 27) to get ready for a big blowout and to get their TV cameras in place. The BATF originally denied it told the media, but later admitted that it had.

2. The BATF said that Koresh had to be arrested at the compound because he had not left it for several months. Numerous people in the area said that was a lie and that they had frequently seen him out jogging, at the store, and in town until shortly before the attack. The BATF finally admitted they knew nothing about Koresh's movements because they NEVER even put him under surveillance, let alone did they try to arrest him.

3. The BATF originally said that they had an arrest warrant for Koresh and a search warrant for the compound. Later it was shown that they only had a search warrant and no arrest warrant.

4. The BATF said that the element of surprise was the key to success and that they wouldn't have attacked if they had known that the Branch Davidians were expecting them. This was a lie. Everyone in town, including the Branch Davidians,

knew about the coming attack. Later BATF director Higgins admitted that they knew they had lost the element of surprise and went ahead with the attack anyway. That decision caused the death of four BATF agents.

5. The BATF told the Texas National Guard (in order to obtain use of their helicopters), that there was an illegal drug lab at the compound. There was no evidence of this before, during, or after the raid according to the *Waco Tribune-Herald* (March 28, 1993).

6. On March 6, FBI officers denied that they had any plans to use psychological warfare techniques against the Branch Davidians (i.e., such as loud rock music, bright lights, weird sounds). The FBI used them constantly throughout the siege.

7. In his press conference the evening of the fire, Bill Clinton said Janet Reno had acted "because of the children" who were "being abused." Later, officials admitted that there was no evidence of child abuse.

8. On March 2, the FBI's Bob Ricks told reporters that when the FBI approached Koresh, he was going to go outside with grenades (in front of the TV cameras), pull the pin, commit suicide, and take as many agents with him as he could. On April 20 on *MacNeil/Lehrer Newshour* FBI director William Sessions said that all of the FBI analyses of Koresh indicated that he would *never* commit suicide.

9. On April 28, FBI deputy director Floyd Clarke told the House Judiciary Committee that the *"Branch Davidians had used their own children as human shields by holding them up in front of the windows."* The truth is, the Branch Davidians hoisted their children up to the windows to see the M1-A1 Abrams battle tanks sitting in their front yard, as FBI spokesman Richard Swensen later admitted.

10. BATF director Stephen Higgins testified before a Senate subcommittee (April 2, 1993) that the BATF mission failed only *"because the Branch Davidians ambushed the BATF."* What a lie. The BATF attacked the Branch Davidians and not the other way around.

11. The FBI and Janet Reno stated repeatedly that the reason they attacked the compound on April 19 was *"concern for the*

safety and well being of the children.'' You don't ram into buildings with military tanks and pump CS gas into a building filled with women and children, and call it ''a concern for the safety of the children.''

12. CS gas was described by Clinton, Reno, and FBI officials as a harmless (irritant) tear gas. *This is a lie!* It is 80 times stronger than tear gas, immobilizes its victims and throws them into violent coughing and convulsions.

13. The government said they had exhausted all avenues to resolve the standoff. *This is a lie!* They refused to let *any* of the family members speak with the Branch Davidians even though this has helped to resolve many such former standoffs. They refused to let ''Bo'' Gritz and Jack McLamb, who negotiated Randy Weaver and his family out last August, assist, although they volunteered numerous times.

14. The BATF said after the February 28 fiasco that *''we were outgunned.'' That was a lie!* They had helicopter gunships, armored vehicles, and fully automatic weapons to use against the Branch Davidians, not to mention stun grenades and the military's most high-tech equipment.

15. On April 19, FBI spokesman Bob Ricks quoted Branch Davidian survivor Renos Avraam as saying: *''The fire's been lit. The fire's been lit.''* But when questioned on camera by reporters, Avraam said, *''One of the tanks knocked over a gas lantern, and it started a fire under some bales of hay that were laying around. . . . The fire wasn't started by us.''*

The Liberal Media Is Cooperating in the Cover-up

The mainline media in America is owned by the Establishment and is by-and-large very pro-Clinton. So, unlike the Rodney King case where they were instantly *for* King and *against* the police, in Waco the media were instantly *for* the BATF and FBI and *against* the Branch Davidians. There has been ''some'' accurate newspaper coverage, but for the most part the media has reported the Clintonista party line on Waco 100 percent, and has totally ignored the Constitutional, due process, and human rights issues.

During *MacNeil/Lehrer News Hour* (April 20, 1993) terrorism ''expert'' Frank McGuire claimed that *''David Koresh had left a trail of criminal behavior going back to 1987''* (which was not true) and Fort Worth

Star-Telegram columnist Bill Thompson described him as *"one of the vilest mass murderers of our time,"* (which also was not true). FBI spokesman Bob Ricks labeled Koresh *"a classical sociopath,"* Attorney General Janet Reno branded him *"a dangerous criminal,"* and Bill Clinton called him *"dangerous, irrational, and probably insane."* Then the media repeated these unsubstantiated (and largely untrue) allegations thousands of times, and to the average American they became "truth." [**Note:** The dynamic duo of government and media have the ability to create "reality," or the "appearance of reality" out of thin air!]

Such unsubstantiated statements served to condition the public to accept the Draconian government response as justified, no matter how unconstitutional and brutal, since the target was characterized as a monster who had to be brought down by any means.

[**Note:** It has occurred to this writer that he has seen *no* pictures of the people killed at Waco, including the children. After a plane crash or other tragedy, pictures of the victims (while alive) are usually shown. Not so with Operation Waco. The pictures might elicit public sympathy (e.g., *these were real people, real children, real babies which were slaughtered*). No pictures are likely to be forthcoming.]

Then shortly after the April 19 inferno, the made-for-TV network movies began to emerge, retelling the government version in gory detail. First came the NBC made-for-TV presentation, which faithfully followed the FBI/BATF/Clintonista party line. According to the May 5, 1993 issue of *Time, before the last bodies were removed from the rubble in Waco an NBC film crew was already recording the re-enactment scenes at the reconstruction of the site in Oklahoma.*

Does anyone really think that a Justice Department investigation of its own FBI, or a Treasury Department investigation of its own BATF will be anything besides a total whitewash? And as for a congressional investigation, Senator Dennis DeConcini (D-AZ), a member of the Senate Judiciary Committee, has already said, regarding a congressional investigation: *"I'm not looking for them to blame anyone or anything like that."* They must cover up and bury the biggest potential political scandal in U.S. history. If Watergate could sink the Nixon Administration, Wacogate, which is 100 times bigger, could certainly sink the Clinton Administration. But it won't-- it will be completely covered up! Watch for disappearing BATF and/or FBI agents who know too much and don't like what they saw, or for strange things happening to Branch Davidian survivors in jail. *Before it is over, the cover-*

up will be thorough, total, and perhaps as deadly as the massacre itself.

More Present Parallels with Nazi Germany:
The Warsaw Ghetto Massacre of April 19, 1943 vs.
the Waco Branch Davidian Massacre of April 19, 1993

In April, this writer analyzed seven parallels between America today and Nazi Germany in 1933. These included:

1. A preoccupation with death;
2. Thousands of laws, rules, and regulations were passed to control every aspect of the German people's lives;
3. There was an occultic dimension to the Third Reich;
4. A preoccupation with animal rights;
5. Ignoring the Constitution;
6. Rejection of their heritage; and
7. The government used homosexuals, drug addicts, and criminal elements to destabilize the country and advance the Nazi political machine.

All of these elements of the Third Reich are present in America today as we move toward the New World Order (which could be called the Fourth Reich). Numbers 1, 2, and 5 were especially evidence in "Operation Waco."

But there are other parallels between Nazi Germany of the 1930s and America of the 1990s. *Gun control was essential to establishing the Third Reich and gun laws were passed in the late 1920s and '30s which led to total confiscation of privately owned firearms in Nazi Germany. Today gun laws are being pushed and passed which are designed to lead to total confiscation over the next three to seven years, which is essential to the establishment of the New World Order/New Age dictatorship. That is what Operation Waco is all about--to accelerate the gun control juggernaut.*

There is another parallel between Nazi Germany in the 1930s and America in the 1990s. *The Third Reich declared "open season" on non-mainstream (i.e., those not controlled by the government) religious minorities which were considered "dangerous misfits." These included Jews, fundamental evangelical Christians, gypsies, and others.* In America today, the Fourth Reich (i.e., the Establishment, the Clintonistas, the New World Order/New Age/environmentalists/pro-gay/pro-choice crowds) have declared "open season" on non-mainstream (non-government approved) religious minorities, sects, etc.--now defined as the smoke clears from Waco as "dangerous religious cults." *Many small Christian churches, communities, and groups are about to be so re-classified.*

This writer believes that among other things, Operation Waco was the beginning of religious persecution of unpopular, non-mainstream religious groups in America. Since the American people (including Christians) did not protest one peep over the destruction of the Branch Davidian sect, the attacks will now begin to accelerate.

Storm Troopers In the U.S.A.

It is an interesting coincidence that the Clintonistas picked the 50th anniversary of the Nazi's raid on the Jewish ghetto, and slaughter of innocents in Warsaw, Poland, to destroy the Waco compound and slaughter the innocents. The parallels between the two events are quite ominous.

On April 19, 1943, black uniformed SS men wearing "coal shuttle" helmets and carrying German-made machine pistols attacked the Jewish compound in Warsaw, Poland. The SS men were searching for illegal weapons reported by a paid informant to be in the Warsaw ghetto prior to the SS assault. A great slaughter of innocent men, women, and children followed.

On April 19, 1993 (exactly 50 years later to the day), black uniformed U.S. government agents wearing "coal scuttle" helmets and carrying German-made machine pistols attacked the Branch Davidian compound in Waco, Texas. (The BATF actually made the first attack 51 days earlier.) The BATF and FBI were searching for illegal weapons reported by a paid informant to be in the Branch Davidian compound. Reports from Waco tell us that the Branch Davidians kept to themselves and harmed no one outside their compound prior to the BATF assault.

Nazi news media (and the Nazi government) told the German people that the Jews practiced contemptible sexual rituals involving young women and children, so they were branded an "evil religion." And the gullible German people believed their government and media and supported the attack. The SS had its propagandists document its assault to show the German public how dangerous the Jews were. Eleven SS men were killed and an unrecorded number wounded in the initial assault on the Warsaw ghetto. (The Jews had been tipped off about the impending assault.)

The U.S. broadcast media (and the Clintonista government) told us that the Branch Davidians practiced contemptible sexual rituals involving young women and children, so they were branded "an evil religious cult."

And the gullible American people believed their government and media and supported the attack. The BATF invited the media to document the assault to show the American people how dangerous the Branch Davidians were. Four BATF men were killed and 16 wounded in the original assault on the compound. (The Davidians had been tipped off about the impending assault.)

After their initial assault, the SS men magnanimously arranged a truce so children could be evacuated from the Warsaw ghetto compound (and they could tend to their casualties). The SS then called up Waffen SS military units with armored vehicles to finish off the Warsaw ghetto after encountering fierce resistance against the initial assault.

After their initial assault, the BATF men magnanimously arranged a truce so children could be evacuated from the Branch Davidian compound (and they could tend to their casualties). The BATF called FBI and U.S. military units with armored vehicles to finish off the Branch Davidian compound after encountering fierce resistance against the initial assault.

The SS personnel stationed in the general government of Poland were trying to improve their image with superiors in Berlin by staging a well-publicized attack upon a politically powerless group. Most of the SS personnel stationed in Poland had been sent there because they had fallen afoul in Nazi political infighting, not because they wanted to contend with an unrelentingly hostile population on a daily basis.

The BATF personnel in Waco were trying to improve their image with the U.S. public by staging a well-publicized attack upon an equally powerless group. Even before BATF was accused of racial and sexual harassment of its own agents on the CBS program *60 Minutes* in early February, they had the worst reputation in U.S. federal law enforcement.

The Waco incident is a clear example of how little respect the U.S. government has for its own Constitution. The BATF not only trampled the politically incorrect Second Amendment, they made a mockery of the First and Fourth Amendments as well. They also trampled one of our most sacred Constitutional rights--freedom of belief (i.e., freedom of religion).

Almost 50 years have passed since Allied forces crushed the Nazis, but their totalitarian philosophy of *Ordnung* is beginning to reappear in the New World Order with all of its police state manifestations. Fifty years have passed, but little has changed. As Santayana once said: *"Those who do not learn from history are doomed to repeat the mistakes of history."*

[**Note:** The information about the Warsaw ghetto vs. the Branch Davidian massacre came from *The Wall Street Journal*, March 15, 1993, in a Letter to the Editor from John D. Dingell, Wyandotte, Michigan.]

The BATF (The New Gestapo) in Action

The BATF is a Treasury Department entity whose early agents made a name chasing moonshiners and bootleggers during the 1920s. It began as a tax collecting agency, but now has law enforcement powers as well. Following passage of the 1968 Gun Control Act, the Alcohol and Tobacco Division of the IRS became the Alcohol, Tobacco, *and Firearms* Division (ATFD). On July 1, 1972, the division was elevated to full bureau status. The BATF has around 2,000 agents and a fiscal 1993 budget of about $350 million.

President Reagan referred to the BATF as *"that rogue agency."* Sen. James McClure (R-ID) has described the BATF as *"an agency that has gone wild."* In 1982 the Senate Judiciary Sub-Committee on the Constitution reported that there was *"little doubt that [the BATF] has disregarded rights guaranteed by the Constitution and the laws of the United States."* The report charged that the BATF

> *". . . trampled upon the Second Amendment by chilling exercise of the right to keep and bear arms by law-abiding citizens and had 'offended' the Fourth Amendment by unreasonably searching and seizing private property. It had ignored the Fifth Amendment by taking property without just compensation and entrapping honest citizens without regard to their due process of law."*

BATF's feeble attempt at rebuttal was, according to the report, *"utterly unconvincing."* The same committee determined that

> *". . . 75 percent of BATF gun prosecutions were aimed at ordinary citizens, who had neither criminal intent nor knowledge, but were enticed by agents into unknowing technical violations."*

The Senate panel report also cited the BATF as guilty of not only violating *"the dictates of common sense,"* but also the federal law banning *"secret law-making"* by administrative bodies. *"These practices . . . leave little doubt that [the BATF] has disregarded rights guaranteed by the Constitution and the laws of the United States. "* The BATF's *"enforcement tactics . . . are constitutionally, illegal, and practically, reprehensible. "* In addition, it noted that the Bureau *"has primarily devoted its firearms enforcement efforts to the apprehension on technical . . . charges of individuals who lack all criminal intent and knowledge. "*

[Note: The above information on the BATF is from *Second Alamo*, by Frank Oresnik.]

Desmond Griffin recently wrote in the *Midnight Messenger* newsletter:

"Although the Waco tragedy is the bloodiest and most tragic event of its kind thus far, the initial raid that led up to it certainly wasn't unique; it was, in fact, just one of thousands of similar raids that have been staged nationwide in recent years by the Bureau of Alcohol, Tobacco, and Firearms (BATF or ATF) and the U.S. Marshals Service.

"Both these branches of government have worked very hard for--and diligently earned--reputations similar to what the monstrously hypocritical liberals love to call the 'jackbooted Nazi hordes' in Hitler's Germany. Tens of thousands coast-to-coast-- in our so-called 'land of the free and home of the brave'--have been traumatized by their terror tactics in recent years (2,000 in 1992 alone).

"The first indication many of these victims had of impending trouble was when their front doors were torn off their hinges by a battering ram and their homes invaded by a teeming horde of camouflaged, armor-clad, hooded, black-booted thugs armed with the most modern automatic and semi-automatic weapons-- all, of course, with the 'authorization' of the runaway federal government.

"David Troy, a BATF intelligence officer, described Branch Davidian leader David Koresh as a 'cheap thug who interpreted the Bible through the barrel of a gun.' However, with its widespread history of terror tactics, many believe the BATF is comprised of a bunch of 'cheap thugs who make and interpret the law through the barrel of a gun.'

"Daily, it seems, such tactics are praised, glorified, and

immortalized by an ever-growing parade of TV programs. Americans are being pressured, intimidated, and coerced into believing that such Gestapo and KGB-like tactics are par for the course and are thus to be accepted as every day occurrences in our once Christian nation.''

Larry Pratt, executive director of Gun Owners of America, recently testified before a congressional hearing where he said, *"These people [BATF] have a history of lying, of killing people . . . clearly it's time to act."* Pratt recounted several recent BATF atrocities:

1. The killing of a mother and child in an attack on a remote Idaho cabin (i.e., Vicki and Sam Weaver);
2. The ransacking and intimidation of a Portland, Oregon woman and her children on a mistaken identity (*Oregonian*, March 7, 1993);
3. The terrorizing of a Washington State woman who was forced to leave her baby unattended in a bathtub for an extended period--all because of the allegations of a known lunatic (April 1, 1992). (There are thousands more examples.)

Alan Bock, the senior columnist for the *Orange County Register*, on April 8, 1993 criticized the BATF for its attack on the Branch Davidians and its repressive agenda.

"Early on in the siege, after it became apparent that the initial raid was casually and thoughtlessly carried out, lots of people criticized the BATF's tactics and even its arrogance. It soon became evident that the thuggish BATF is the pond scum of federal law enforcement agencies. But too few dug a little deeper to question whether the raid was, in any sense, justified.

"The Branch Davidians are pretty strange, no doubt. But so far the BATF has produced no evidence that they constitute a danger to their neighbors--whom they left alone peacefully--or to anyone in the Waco area, let alone in the rest of the United States. Why was this obscure religious minority subjected to undercover informants paid for with your tax dollars?

"To date there's still no solid evidence that the BATF even

had good reason to believe the compound contained illegal weapons. The best conjecture now is that the BATF sought a conspicuous enforcement action against a tiny and despised religious minority to make its cowboy agents look like heroes."

What About the FBI?

The FBI, executor of the final siege and massacre in Waco, has come a long way since the heroic days of J. Edgar Hoover. As one editorialist put it, *"the FBI has obviously fallen on bad times when it starts the day by gassing women and children."* The FBI did not make its considerable reputation by fighting old women and children, but the agency of J. Edgar Hoover's highly vaunted G-men lost it in Waco at the hands of dead women and children on a Central Texas prairie. *Today's FBI is not at all the same FBI that many of us grew up idolizing--its leaders, personnel, and philosophy have completely changed.*

Since J. Edgar Hoover's sudden and unexplained death in the mid-'70s, the FBI has been sliding progressively into the hands of the Establishment. Instead of fighting to preserve freedom by opposing communism, organized crime, etc., it is now being used to extinguish freedom by monitoring the actions of the American people (i.e., it wants to monitor all Americans' phone calls) and attacking Americans with military force, as in the Weaver case and in the Waco massacre. The FBI currently has a budget of $2 billion and 10,366 agents, who are rapidly becoming part of Bill Clinton's national police force.

Questions That Need To Be Raised and Answered

1. **Why** didn't the BATF apprehend David Koresh outside of the compound? Local press reports indicate that he jogged outside regularly and ate at a local restaurant.

2. **What** crimes did Koresh and the Branch Davidians commit that justified the storming of a compound where women and children would be put at risk? If the alleged crime was a weapons violation, what implications does this hold for tens of thousands of gun owners who are not complying with the "assault weapons" bans around the country? (There are over 300,000 such individuals in California alone.) Will the BATF assault or invade their homes and shoot and/or burn them as

well? (Indeed, they did invade 2,000 homes or businesses last year.)

3. **Why** is the BATF not focusing its efforts on truly violent gangs which are well armed and have even driven out the Mafia in some cases?

4. **Why** didn't the BATF send out two county sheriff's officers to serve Koresh and the Branch Davidians with a search warrant as had happened before? He complied and cooperated before, and it is believed by local Waco officials that he would have this time as well.

5. **Why** in July '92, when the BATF checked a local gun store and found records of Branch Davidian gun purchases, and the store owner called Koresh to tell them of the BATF in his store (at that moment), and Koresh invited the BATF agents to come out to the compound and check around for themselves, did the BATF agents decline Koresh's offer? The store owner, Henry McMahon, has told this story to the press in detail. *He noted that Koresh was always meticulous in filling out the proper paperwork for his gun purchases.*

6. **Why** did the FBI call the Waco hospitals and tell them to get ready for a large number of burn victims six hours or more before the fire broke out if they didn't know a fire would be ignited?

7. **Why** did the FBI *send* fire trucks (which had been stationed near the compound for seven weeks) away and *keep* them away throughout the assault on April 19? They had to know that smashing holes in the side of the building could ignite a fire. *Why didn't they call the fire trucks until 30 minutes after the fire broke out and why did they prevent the firemen from fighting the fire for still another hour?* The fire chief said that he was standing by but they didn't call him. Why?

8. **Why** did the FBI wait for a day when the winds were blowing 40 mph--obviously a high fire risk day and the first such since the siege began 51 days earlier?

9. **Why** did the FBI keep all local law enforcement people and Texas Rangers away from the Mt. Carmel site after the holocaust, and then bulldoze away the evidence three weeks later on May 12? What were they trying to hide?

10. **Did** an FBI "special ops" team fire the bullets into Koresh and Schneider and other Branch Davidian leaders after they were already dead to make it look like they committed suicide?

11. **Could** the men in black the FBI sniper said he saw through his scope inside the compound just before the fire broke out have been a "special ops" team sent in to take out the Branch Davidian leaders while making it appear that they committed suicide, and also have been sent in to light the fires? The sniper said he saw men in black setting fires. Such teams operated very effectively in southern Iraq for weeks before Operation Desert Storm. How about Waco?

12. **Why** would Koresh and his leaders have donned black uniforms just as the assault began? Koresh *never* wore black, but the BATF, FBI, and "special ops" forces do. Is this why the press and fire department were kept away--to cover that team's escape from the compound? Is this why the burnt out complex was put off limits to all local and state authorities, and to the press, and to all authorities except the FBI and BATF, and then bulldozed? What were they trying to hide by bulldozing the site?

These are all questions that a "legitimate" investigation should ask, but there is not likely to be a "legitimate" investigation, nor are most of these questions (and many more) likely to ever be asked or answered.

Chapter Four

The Coming Persecution of Christians, Traditionalists, and Constitutionalists in America

"I hope very much that others who will be tempted to join cults . . . will be deterred by the horrible scenes they have seen over the past seven weeks" (President Bill Clinton, April 19, 1993).

Operation Waco was about gun control, but it was also about silencing "crazy religious nuts" called "dangerous religious cultists." Another purpose of the Waco siege was to make all small and independent churches who believe in the return of the Lord Jesus Christ suspect.

In the wake of the February 27 attack on the Branch Davidians, the Establishment press has begun to define for us how to recognize dangerous religious cultists: they have a preoccupation with Jesus Christ (and especially His Second Coming); with Bible prophecy; with Jerusalem; with Bible studies; they are often home schoolers; they believe in spanking their children ("child abuse"); they believe in survival food, self-sufficiency, and guns.

In short, the new emerging definition of a "dangerous religious cultist" includes millions of Christians, traditionalists, and Constitutionalists. And it should be remembered that the New World Order/New Age crowd, the homosexuals, the environmentalists, the pro-abortion crowd, the women's libbers, the secular humanists, and the occult (in short, the people who dominate the American government, media, and educational system today) are *all very hostile to fundamental evangelical Christians.*

The words "cult" and "sect" (connoting evil) were used continuously by the media throughout the Waco siege to prejudice still further the minds of the public. "Cult" is by "new" definition a religion the government and Establishment don't approve of. *This could be the beginning of an effort to increasingly turn the minds of the public against anyone who holds deep religious convictions. President Clinton has warned people everywhere to stay out of small religious groups. The insinuation is that only big mainstream churches (which can be controlled through disallowance of tax write-offs and other forms of intimidation) can be trusted.*

In Russia, Romania, and elsewhere in the East bloc, there was the above ground church which was spiritually neutral, collaborated with the government, and was infiltrated and controlled by the KGB. Then there was the smaller, underground, persecuted church of true followers of God. *It seems that something similar is emerging in the United States in the 1990s. Over the next three to seven years thousands of small home churches are likely to emerge where people can quietly practice their faith without being called "child abusers," "homophobes," and "dangerous cultists."*

It should be noted that in the first century, followers of Christ throughout the Roman Empire were known as a dangerous "sect" that was "everywhere spoken against" (Acts 28:22) and believed to be spreading superstitions and ideas that were against the best interests of the state. Today as the state increasingly expands its claim to "godhood," history could repeat itself. Bible believers would do well to pay attention to the danger signals.

In Nazi Germany, when the persecution of Jews, Christians, gypsies, and small religious sects began, it began very quickly, like a whirlwind. On July 20, 1937 the SS Reichfuehrer Reinhard Heydrich ordered the banning and persecution of small religious sects, including the Seventh Day Adventists. [Note: The Branch Davidians were an offshoot of the Seventh Day Adventists.] The persecution accelerated rapidly from that point forward.

A Very Dangerous Book

A very important book has come out which is being widely quoted in the Establishment media to point out the danger to Americans from fundamental evangelical Bible/prophecy-believing Christians. *When Time Shall Be No More: Prophecy Belief in Modern American Culture* by Paul Boyer, a professor of history at the University of Wisconsin, is being widely quoted in the *New York Times, USA Today,* etc.

It analyzes the American fundamental/evangelical movement with special emphasis on "prophecy freaks." The analysis is thorough and in many respects accurate, but the conclusions are deadly. Christians are the "root of all evil" in America: they were (or are) responsible for the arms race, the cold war, poverty, child abuse, homophobia, and practically everything bad in America. They are far more powerful than most casual observers ever thought and have Machiavellian designs for control of America.

This book could become the intellectual basis for the coming persecution of Christians in America. Anyone who is concerned or troubled by such things should get this book, read it, and ponder its implications. The political left and those groups in America who hate Christians are studying it closely.

The Ominous Cult Awareness Network (CAN)

Headed by Patricia Ryan, daughter of Rep. Leon Ryan, the San Francisco congressman who was murdered in Jonestown, Guyana in 1979, CAN kidnaps about 500 people a year from cult groups and de-programs them using brainwashing techniques not dissimilar from those used by the cults themselves. CAN has established itself as the "expert authority" on cult activities in the U.S., giving it great authority and influence with law enforcement agencies involved in "anti-cult" activity.

CAN apparently "alerted" the BATF that the Branch Davidians were a "dangerous religious cult" headed for a Jonestown-style mass suicide and "demanded" almost a year ago that government action be taken. CAN advised the BATF before and during the Waco siege as "cult experts." Patricia Ryan was quoted in the *Houston Post* on April 9 as saying that the FBI should use any means possible to arrest Koresh, *"even lethal force."*

[Note: CAN should not be confused by Christians with genuine anti-cult Christian groups such as the one run by the late Walter Martin. CAN is likely to become a major element in the coming Christian persecution in America--equating many non-mainstream sects, cults, and Christian groups with one another and labeling *all* as "dangerous religious cults."]

CAN "experts" advised the BATF and FBI throughout the siege on the Branch Davidians' dangerous "child abuse," "their tendency toward mass suicide," "their end of the world/Armageddon/self-destruct psychosis," etc. Much of what the government said about the Branch Davidians during the siege originated with CAN. One of CAN's techniques is to produce reports from former members of a cult, sect, or religious group who have gone through the CAN *de*-programming (or is it *re*-programming) at the hands of the CAN "mind control" experts. These allegations usually include child and sexual abuse, mass destruction, etc.

As the *Los Angeles Times* editorialist Alexander Cockburn wrote (April 21, 1993): *"The role in Waco of Cult Awareness Network, whose members are respectfully cited in the press as 'experts' may well have been crucial.''* He describes the strong influence on Waco events by CAN, and says: *"CAN has a long history of persecution of what it deems to be cults.''*

On May 13, 1993, Patricia Ryan authored an article entitled ''Are Other Waco's Waiting to Happen?'' for the *Los Angeles Times.* She wrote:

> *"The general reaction of the public has been to distance itself from the tragedy in Waco, Tex., as if the deaths of the Branch Davidian cultists were merely a minor blemish on the face of American society. However, if we place Waco in a wider context of how extremist groups function in this country, we may find a festering infection not easily dismissed.''*

She goes on to discuss the *''common threads''* of child abuse, guns, suicide drills, fanatical religious beliefs, political extremism, etc., and says:

> *"If we don't look closely, we will not be able to truly determine how many of these common threads are, in fact, being woven through the fabric of American society.''*

Rumors abound that the government is next targeting (with the help of CAN) the Church Universal and Triumphant headed by Elizabeth Clare Prophet. *Many Christians might say, what does it matter to me if the government takes down sects, cults, or weirdos who are not truly Christian. Go back and ponder the first quote on page one. They are rapidly expanding the definition of ''dangerous religious cult'' to include any religious minority that may be anti-Establishment or non-mainstream, or which may oppose the New World Order.*

Why should we care if the government decimates the Branch Davidians (their constitutional rights, property, and lives)? First, because it is wrong and violates the U.S. Constitution. Second, because the men, women, and children the government slaughtered in Waco were fellow Americans who had a right to live in spite of their weird beliefs. And, third, because you or your group could be next!

Conclusion

There *is* a black cloud rolling across the land. We are being moved irresistibly toward a socialist police state with many of the trappings of communist Russia and Nazi Germany. Operation Waco was a watershed event in the history of America--the greatest example of police state power in our history--and televised on prime time for the entertainment of the masses. *It was also an example of America's new national police force in action.*

America is a nation of sheep--unthinking, soft people who have forgotten the principles (and the God) which made us a great nation. We are a people in moral and spiritual decline who can no longer recognize the difference between good and evil--let alone, as a people, oppose that evil. The average American cannot even look at the atrocity which was just perpetrated by our government in the massacre at Waco and see that it was raw, unadulterated evil. Indeed, Janet Reno is now seen as the new "folk hero" in Washington for having courageously won the "shootout at the Waco corral."

Why should a nation of people who cannot see anything wrong with the murder of 30 million babies in their mothers' wombs object to the extermination of almost 100 "religious fanatics who obviously had weird ideas about religion and guns"? Why should the average American care when some "gun nut," "pro-life freak," "tax rebel," "religious fanatic," or "survivalist" is beaten, jailed, has his property seized, or is killed?

After all, this doesn't affect the average American, sitting smugly in his comfort zone in suburbia, who would never be a part of one of those weirdo groups which the government is going after. But it *will* affect the average American--and a lot sooner than he thinks.

Meanwhile, since the Establishment senses less resistance to their plans than ever, and believes that with the Clintonistas now in the White House and their machinery for socialism and world government now firmly in place, that it is time to "go for broke." In the days, weeks, and months ahead, the government is going to begin to bring strong pressure to bear against traditionalists, Constitutionalists, Christians, gun owners, pro-lifers, and other resistors to their vision of a "New (socialist) America."

In the wake of Operation Waco (which in some ways was a test case) and the total lack of response or protest from the American people or the religious community (after all--who would speak up for "weirdos"), the Clintonistas now have carte blanche for escalating their attacks against these resistor (dissident) types, non-mainstream "fringe" groups and individuals. *The persecution of the remnant has begun!*

What To Do

If you are already a member of the remnant, you need to be moving toward self-sufficiency and less dependence upon the system as rapidly as possible. You need to be getting out of harm's way. The financial/political/social system in America is going to hit the wall over the next three to five years in ways heretofore unimaginable. Are you and your family prepared? Most Americans, including those in the remnant, are not!

Avoid direct confrontation with the government! As Waco proved, the government will overwhelm their opposition in a most dramatic way in direct confrontations. Also, avoid breaking any government laws or regulations. Also, as much as possible, keep a very low profile about your beliefs, your preparations, your guns, gold, survival food, etc. Neighbors and others with "no need to know" might decide to try to "participate in" your preparations, or to turn you in, for a finder's (or informer's) fee for being a "dangerous dissident, or hoarder, or gun owner, etc."

Eight areas of greater self-sufficiency which concerned Americans should be focusing on in the months and years which lie ahead are:

1. Acquisition of basic skills (i.e., hunting, fishing, organic gardening, carpentry, auto mechanics, backpacking, mountain biking, sewing, canning, food preservation, etc.);
2. Acquisition of survival foods;
3. Travel flexibility--have an up-to-date passport for each member of the family;
4. Medical self-sufficiency;
5. Educational self-sufficiency;
6. Reading self-sufficiency;
7. Spiritual self-sufficiency; and
8. Financial self-sufficiency.

If you do not simply want to be a number and a serf in the cashless, computerized New World Order system, if you want to control your children, your family, and your destiny, and if you want to be free, you must expand yourself in these areas of self-sufficiency.

And if you want to remain free, you must get politically involved now. There are excellent political groups which are trying to "stand in the gap" and "turn the tide" (i.e., the U.S. Taxpayers Party, the Conservative Caucus, the John Birch Society, Gun Owners of America, the National Rifle Association, Eagle Forum, Concerned Women for America, Operation Rescue, and hundreds more). Get involved with some of these now!

Chapter Five

Final Thought

America (and most of the world) has entered a period of political, financial, and moral crisis which is likely to be highly convulsive over the next three to seven years. We appear to be entering a period which will "try the souls of men (and women)." *The blindness and apathy are actually growing among many Christians, conservatives, and people who should know better.* As 2 Thessalonians 2:9-12 says:

> *"Even him, whose coming is after the working of Satan with all power and signs and lying wonders, And with all <u>deceivableness</u> of unrighteousness in them that perish; because <u>they received not the love of the truth</u>, that they might be saved. <u>And for this cause God shall send them strong delusion, that they should believe a lie</u>: That they all might be damned who believed not the truth, but had pleasure in unrighteousness."*

But, as Psalm 32:7 says:

> *"<u>Thou art my hiding place</u>; thou shalt preserve me from trouble; thou shalt compass me about with songs of deliverance. Selah."*

The God of the Bible will protect, strengthen, guide, and hide His people even in the midst of the storm. As this writer has long believed, we are in a spiritual as well as a political/financial battle in America and elsewhere. As Ephesians 6:12 says:

> *"For we wrestle not against flesh and blood, but against principalities, against powers, against the rulers of the darkness of this world, against spiritual wickedness in high places."*

Psalm 91 sums up how the Lord will be our "hiding place," our "refuge" and "strength" in times of turmoil. This writer encourages the reader to ponder that Psalm (as well as Psalm 37 and many others) as our world seems to be spinning out of control, because God *is* still in control, and He has the answers!

"He that dwelleth in the secret place of the most High shall abide under the shadow of the Almighty. I will say of the Lord, He is my refuge and my fortress: my God; in him will I trust. Surely he shall deliver thee from the snare of the fowler, and from the noisome pestilence. He shall cover thee with his feathers, and under his wings shalt thou trust: his truth shall be thy shield and buckler. Thou shalt not be afraid for the terror by night; nor for the arrow that flieth by day; Nor for the pestilence that walketh in darkness; nor for the destruction that wasteth at noonday. A thousand shall fall at thy side, and ten thousand at thy right hand; but it shall not come nigh thee. Only with thine eyes shalt thou behold and see the reward of the wicked. Because thou hast made the Lord, which is my refuge, even the most High, thy habitation; There shall no evil befall thee, neither shall any plague come nigh thy dwelling. For he shall give his angels charge over thee, to keep thee in all thy ways. They shall bear thee up in their hands, lest thou dash thy foot against a stone. Thou shalt tread upon the lion and adder: the young lion and the dragon shalt thou trample under feet. Because he hath set his love upon me, therefore will I deliver him: I will set him on high, because he hath known my name. He shall call upon me, and I will answer him: I will be with him in trouble; I will deliver him, and honour him. With long life will I satisfy him, and shew him my salvation."

The Lord is still in control! And that is the bottom line!

Get ready for a new world order!

- How will it affect you?
- How is it happening?
- How can you prepare to protect yourself politically, religiously, and financially?

ISBN 0-9624517-9-7   370 page book

For ordering information,
call or write:
Southwest Radio Church
P.O. Box 1144 ● Oklahoma City, OK 73101
(405) 235-5396 ● (800) 652-1144 ● FAX (405) 236-4634

Other Books on the New World Order

Doorway to Darkness
by Kathleen Hayes

Are governments toppling or are they involved in the painful process of reorganizing? This book shows how the world is reshaping as the New World Order comes closer.

B-786—55 page book

The Fourth Reich: Toward an American Police State
by Don McAlvany

America, in 1993, is plunging toward becoming a socialist police state, remarkably similar to Nazi Germany in the 1930s. Find out why.

B-810—50 page book

President Clinton Will Continue the New World Order
by Dr. Dennis L. Cuddy

Because the term "New World Order" is associated with George Bush, some feel it is now a discarded concept since Bill Clinton has won the presidency. However, the concept of the New World Order is alive and well under the presidency of Bill Clinton.

B-805—50 page book

Triad of Evil
by Bill Uselton

Those who know of Bill Uselton are already aware that he is not only a history teacher, but also an astute observer of political movements in contemporary times. Bill is convinced that as this generation moves toward the termination of the twentieth century, there will be an increasing world clamor for a super-government to be headed by a super-deceiver.

S-793—87 page book

For ordering information, please call 1-800-652-1144